STUDY GUIDES

Science

Year 4

Alan Jarvis and
William Merrick

RISING STARS

Rising Stars UK Ltd, 22 Grafton Street, London W1S 4EX

www.risingstars-uk.com

Published 2007

Design: HL Studios

Illustrations: Bookmatrix (Beehive Illustration)

Editorial project management: Dodi Beardshaw

Editorial: Marieke O'Connor

Cover design: Burville-Riley Design

British Library Cataloguing in Publication Data.

A CIP record for this book is available from the British Library.

ISBN: 978-1-84680-102-0

Printed by: Gutenberg Press, Malta

Contents

How to get the best out of this book

Each topic spreads across two pages and focuses on one major idea. Many of your lessons may be based on these topics. Each double page helps you keep **On track** and **Aiming higher**.

Title and key ideas: tell you what you are aiming to learn. The second idea is always more difficult than the first.

Key information: sets out the key facts that you need to know and the ideas you need to understand fully.

Key questions: The information in this section helps you learn more facts and understand the science in each topic. The investigations you do will give you the evidence you need to prove the scientific facts you've learnt.

Key words and their meanings: help build up your scientific vocabulary. Remember that some words mean one thing in everyday life and something more special in science.

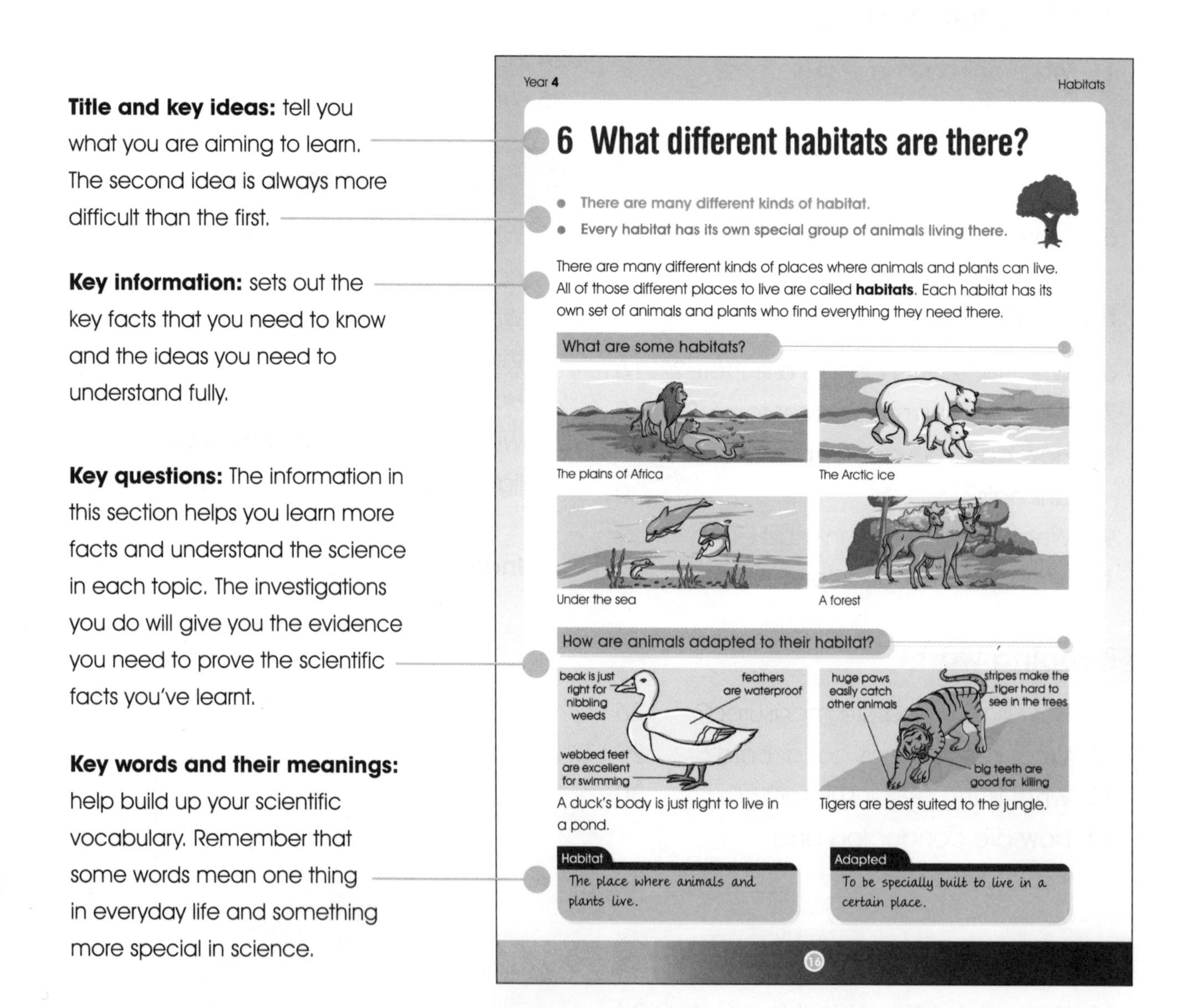
Year **4** Habitats

6 What different habitats are there?

- There are many different kinds of habitat.
- Every habitat has its own special group of animals living there.

There are many different kinds of places where animals and plants can live. All of those different places to live are called **habitats**. Each habitat has its own set of animals and plants who find everything they need there.

What are some habitats?

The plains of Africa

The Arctic ice

Under the sea

A forest

How are animals adapted to their habitat?

beak is just right for nibbling weeds

feathers are waterproof

webbed feet are excellent for swimming

A duck's body is just right to live in a pond.

huge paws easily catch other animals

stripes make the tiger hard to see in the trees

big teeth are good for killing

Tigers are best suited to the jungle.

Habitat
The place where animals and plants live.

Adapted
To be specially built to live in a certain place.

16

Follow these simple rules if you are using the book for revising.

1. Read each page carefully. Give yourself time to take in each idea.
2. Learn the key facts and ideas. Ask your teacher or mum, dad or the adult who looks after you if you need help.
3. Concentrate on the things you find more difficult.
4. Only work for about 20 minutes or so at a time. Take a break and then do more work.

The right-hand page has lots of fun questions for you to try. They are like the National Curriculum test questions you will do. The answers are in the pull-out section in the middle of this book.

If you get most of the **On track** questions right, then you know you are working at level 3. Well done – that's brilliant! If you get most of the **Aiming higher** questions right, you are working at the higher level 4. You're really doing well!

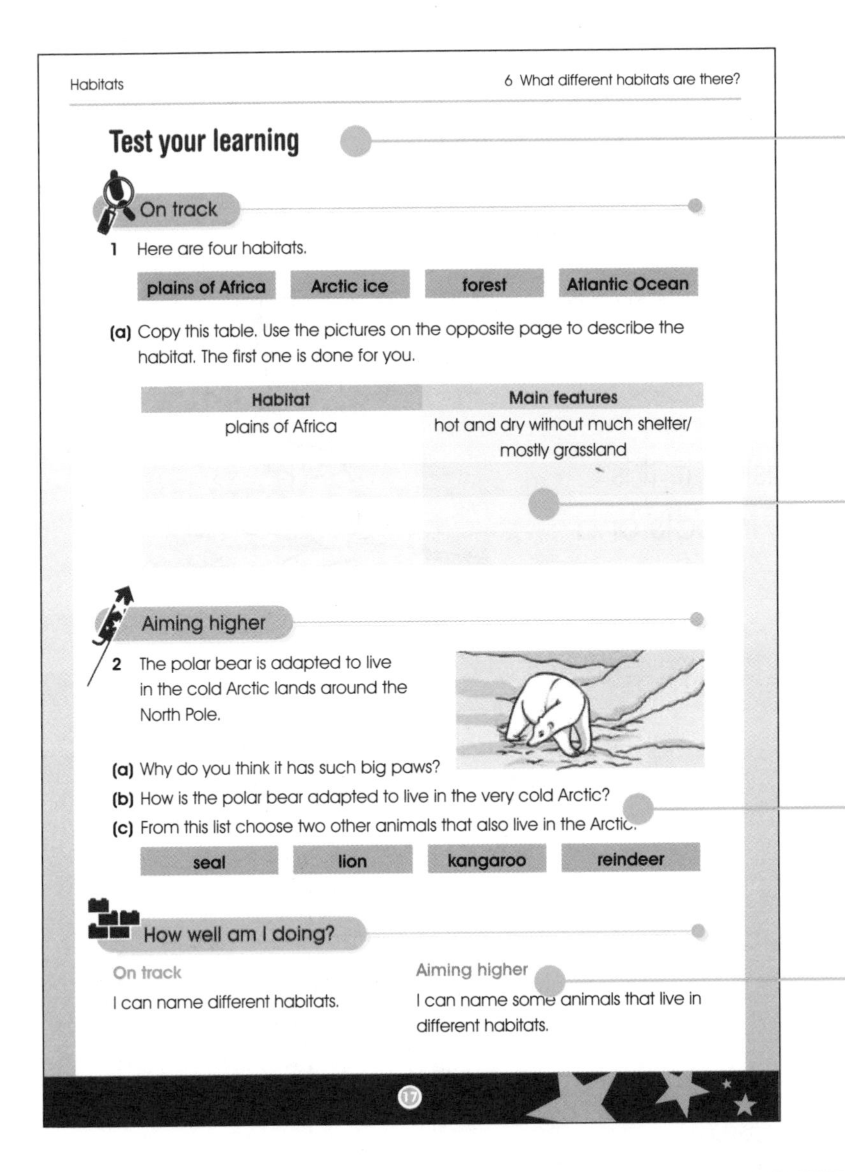

Habitats — 6 What different habitats are there?

Test your learning

On track

1 Here are four habitats.

plains of Africa | Arctic ice | forest | Atlantic Ocean

(a) Copy this table. Use the pictures on the opposite page to describe the habitat. The first one is done for you.

Habitat	Main features
plains of Africa	hot and dry without much shelter/ mostly grassland

Aiming higher

2 The polar bear is adapted to live in the cold Arctic lands around the North Pole.

(a) Why do you think it has such big paws?

(b) How is the polar bear adapted to live in the very cold Arctic?

(c) From this list choose two other animals that also live in the Arctic.

seal | lion | kangaroo | reindeer

How well am I doing?

On track	Aiming higher
I can name different habitats.	I can name some animals that live in different habitats.

17

SAT-style questions: Each question helps you find out how well you have understood what you have learnt. There are questions on facts, ideas and scientific investigations. If you are stuck, the information on the left-hand page will help. **Write all your answers in your notebook.**

On track questions: come in different styles. Be sure to read each one carefully. Think about what the diagrams are telling you.

Aiming higher questions: are more difficult. To answer them well, you have to know more facts or understand a harder idea.

How well am I doing?: helps you to find out the level at which you are working. Keep a running record so you keep on target.

Follow these simple rules if you want to know how well you are doing.

1. Work through the questions.
2. Keep a record of how well you do.
3. If you are working at level 3 you will get most of the **On track** questions correct.
4. If you are working at level 4 you will also get most of the **Aiming higher** questions correct.

1 What animals have skeletons?

- Some animals have skeletons, others don't.
- Skeletons from different animals can be similar.

The human skeleton is made of bone. It keeps us in shape, and helps us to move. Imagine trying to run without your leg bones! The ribs also protect our heart and lungs, and the brain is kept safe inside the skull.

Do all animals have bony skeletons inside them?

Rabbits are **vertebrates**. This means they have a skeleton inside them. Birds, snakes, frogs and fish are also vertebrates.

The snail hasn't got a skeleton inside it. It is called an **invertebrate**. Worms, insects and spiders are also invertebrates.

Can we compare different skeletons?

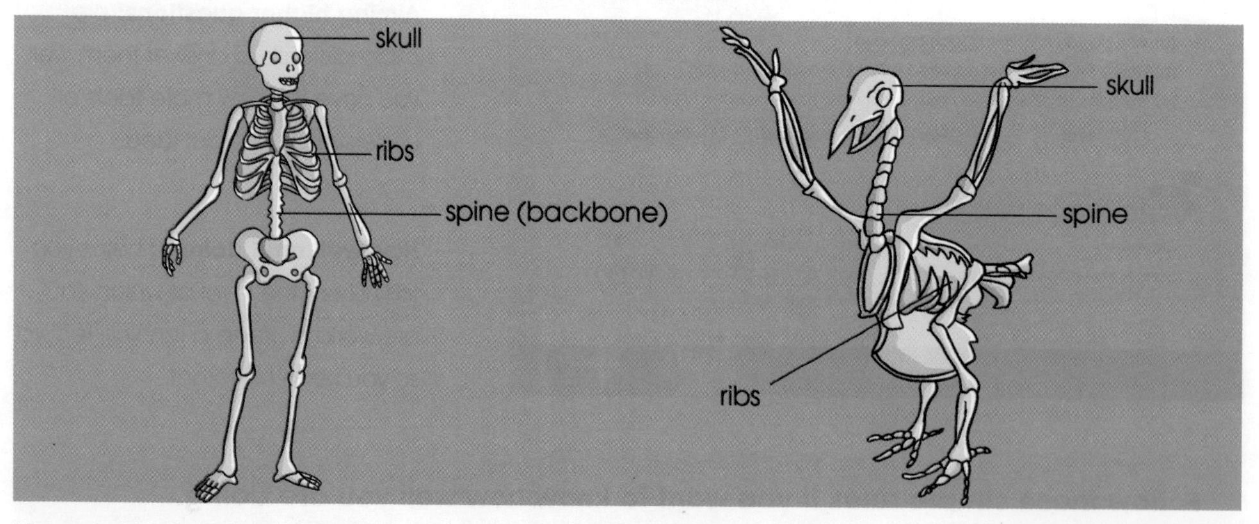

You can see that both skeletons have the same bones – just the shapes are different. The bones inside a bird's wing are very much like the bones in a human arm!

Spine
The bones that run down your back.

Vertebrate
An animal with a bony spine.

Test your learning

On track

1 Nathan's cat has brought a worm in from the garden.

(a) Complete these two sentences using the words in the box.

The cat has a (1)______________ and is a (2)______________ .

The worm does not have bones inside it and is an (3)______________ .

vertebrate **invertebrate** **skeleton**

(b) Here are the names of some vertebrates and invertebrates. Copy the table and put the names of the animals into the right column.

cow **snail** **octopus** **horse** **slug** **eagle**

Vertebrates	Invertebrates

Aiming higher

2 This is a frog skeleton. Look carefully at its back leg bones.

You can see they look the same as human bones, but the shapes and sizes are different.

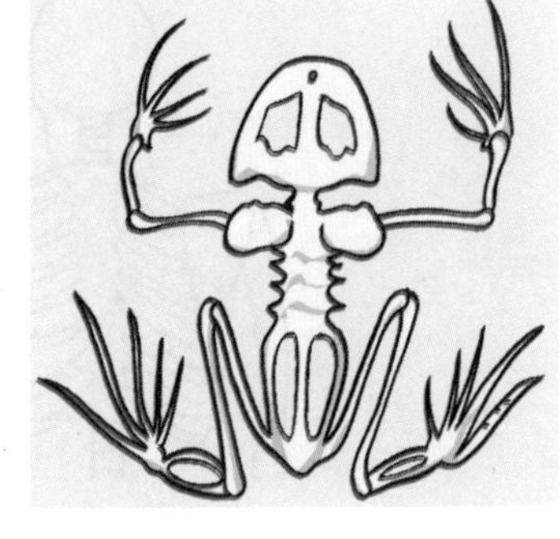

(a) Describe two ways that the frog's leg bones are different to human ones.

(b) How do the frog's special legs help him to move?

How well am I doing?

On track

I can name some animals with or without skeletons.

Aiming higher

I can say how the skeletons of different animals vary.

2 What are bones like?

- **Bones are hard and strong, especially if they carry a lot of weight.**
- **Bones have special places for muscles to hold onto.**

Bones are very strong but they will break if they have too much weight put on them. Some animals (like fish and garden birds) only need small, thin bones. Bigger animals (like cows and horses) need really thick, strong bones.

How strong are bones?

Fish bones do not need to carry much weight. They are thin and bendy.

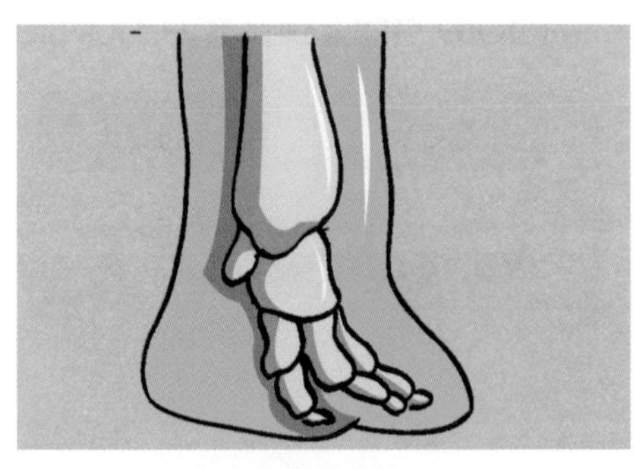

An elephant's foot carries a lot of weight. The bones are very thick and strong.

Can we compare different skeletons?

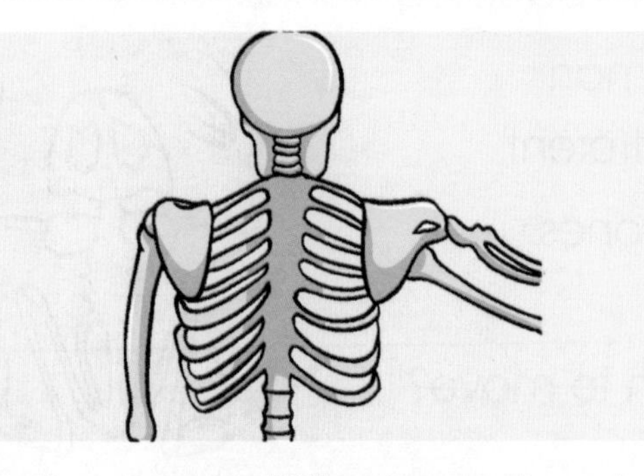

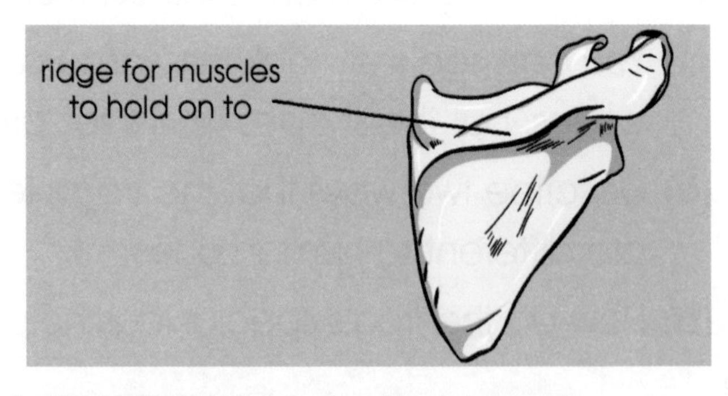

Bones have specially shaped parts that **muscles** join onto. The ridge is easy to see on a shoulder blade, but you can find muscle ridges on lots of different bones.

X-ray photograph
A picture that shows your bones inside you.

Strength
How much weight something can carry before it breaks.

Test your learning

On track

1 Jessica saw a horse skeleton in the museum. Its bones were so much thicker than those of a child!

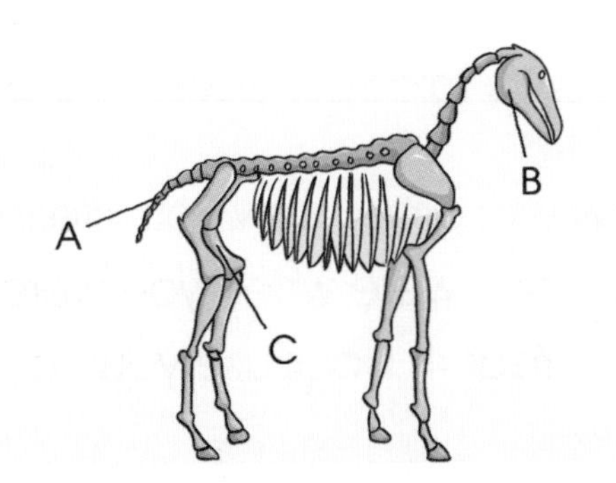

(a) Which bone is carrying the most weight: A, B or C?

(b) Why do you think the horse's leg bones have to be so thick?

Aiming higher

2 Jessica also looked at a gorilla skull and a human skull.

She noticed the large ridge along the top of the gorilla skull, which reminded her of the ridge on a shoulder blade.

The human skull didn't have one at all. It was smooth.

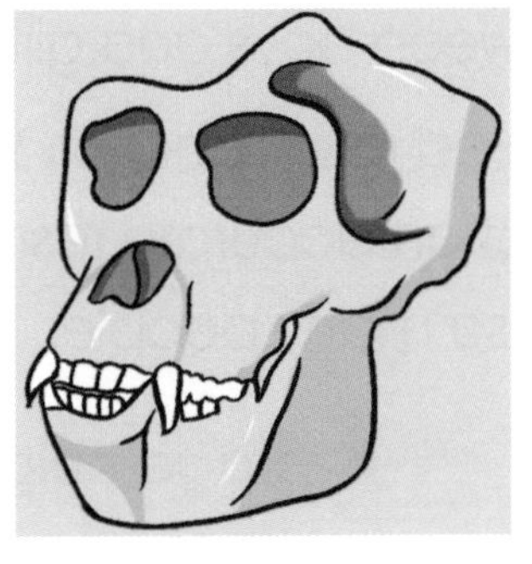

gorilla skull

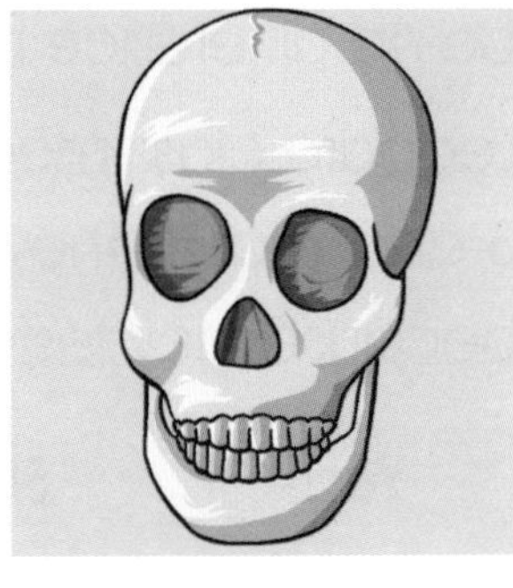

human skull

(a) Complete the following using these words:

muscles **tough** **ridge** **strong**

Gorillas eat very (1)________ food. They need very (2)________ jaw muscles, so they have a big (3)________ on their heads for the (4)________ to hold on to.

How well am I doing?

On track

I can say why some animals have stronger bones than others.

Aiming higher

I can give a reason why some bones have special ridges on them.

3 How fast does your skeleton grow?

- You need to take many measurements to get a reliable result.
- You can use your results to see if your prediction was right.

Your bones get longer as you grow. Now you are in Year 4, your bones will probably be longer than they were when you were in Year 3. You might have needed bigger shoes for Year 4, because your feet have grown so much!

How many measurements should you take in a test?

Mr Sharma's Leopard class wanted an answer to this question: "How much do we grow between Year 3 and Year 4?"

The class also made a prediction. "There will be no difference between boys and girls."

Leopard class measured everybody in Year 3 and Year 4. They got an accurate result because they tested so many people.

Year	Sex	Average height
Year 3	boys	125 cm
Year 3	girls	125 cm
Year 4	boys	130 cm
Year 4	girls	130 cm

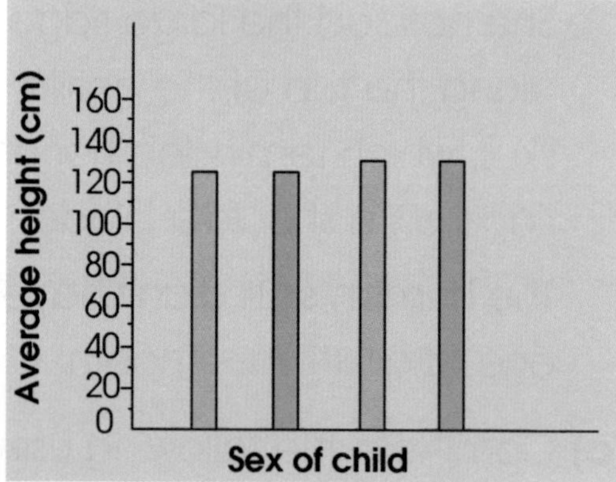

The average height increased from 125 cm in Year 3 to 130 cm in Year 4, so Mr Sharma said: "Children grow an average of 5 cm between Year 3 and Year 4."

Did Leopard class's results show their prediction was right or wrong?

Their prediction was right. Mr Sharma said: "There is no difference between boys and girls."

Prediction

What you think you might discover before you start your experiment.

Bar chart

A way of showing your measurements as a picture.

Test your learning

On track

1 Nathan and his friends were making paper hats. They were measuring round their heads to see how big the hats should be.

Name	Head measurement
Ewan	41 cm
Dominic	45 cm
Aidan	49 cm
Cecilia	43 cm
Nathan	47 cm

(a) Who had the smallest head?

(b) Who had the biggest head?

(c) Which head size was average?

41 cm **45 cm** **47 cm**

Aiming higher

2 Here are three more experiments done by Mr Sharma's class:

- **Experiment 1** Measure the hands of ten children and ten grown-ups.
- **Experiment 2** Measure the height of ten children and ten grown-ups.
- **Experiment 3** Measure the height of ten Year 4 boys and ten Year 4 girls.

Here are three predictions:

- **Prediction 1** "Boys are taller than girls."
- **Prediction 2** "Grown-ups are taller than children."
- **Prediction 3** "Grown-ups have longer finger bones than children."

(a) Match up the right prediction with the right experiment.

How well am I doing?

On track

I can find the average of a few measurements.

Aiming higher

I can use my results to decide if my prediction was right.

4 How do muscles move bones?

- **We can move because our muscles pull on our bones.**
- **Some muscles bend our joints and other muscles straighten them.**

In spooky films you often see skeletons walking along, which is silly – a skeleton can't move at all, unless it has muscles pulling the bones. Feel your arm muscles with your hand; you can feel them pulling as you move your arm.

How do muscles move our bones?

The muscle on top of the footballer's leg has **pulled** his leg straight. Muscles always work by pulling.

Shooting for goal!

How do muscles work together?

Muscles always work together in pairs. They work opposite to each other. You have one muscle to **bend** your arm, and another one to **straighten** it. Your leg is the same.

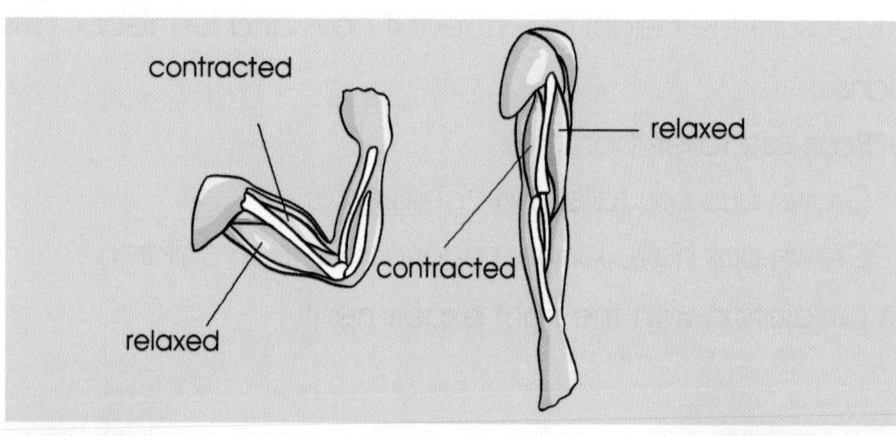

When one muscle **contracts**, the opposite one **relaxes**. This is to let the one that is pulling do its job properly.

Contract

To shorten – muscles contract when they pull on a bone.

Relax

Muscles relax when they stop pulling and stretch back to their original length.

Test your learning

On track

1 Mina is lifting a weight by bending her arm.

(a) Which part of her arm is moving the bones?

skin | blood | muscles | veins

(b) When she bends her arm, is the muscle on the front of her arm pushing or pulling?

Aiming higher

2 You use muscles when you exercise.

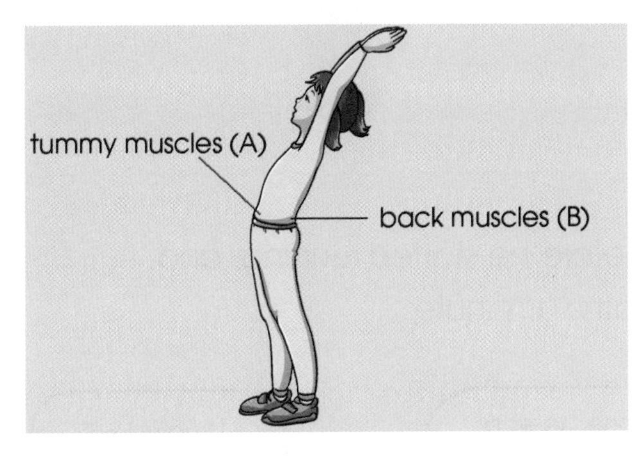

Mina is pulling herself right back.

Now she is bending forward to touch her toes.

(a) When she pulls herself back:

- which main muscles are contracting and pulling?
- which main muscles are relaxing and stretching?

(b) Explain what the muscles do when she bends forward.

How well am I doing?

On track

I can explain that bones move when muscles pull on them.

Aiming higher

I can explain how pairs of muscles bend and straighten joints.

5 How do muscles help you exercise?

- **Exercise makes us get hot and out of breath. Our muscles feel tired.**
- **You need to take a few measurements in every test you do.**

When your muscles work hard they make a lot of heat. Your whole body feels hot, and you sweat to cool down. Your muscles need more oxygen if you are working hard, so you breathe a lot faster.

What happens when we exercise?

Nathan had been running. He noted these changes in his body.

- He was hot and sweating.
- He was breathing very fast.
- His muscles felt tired.

Is one measurement enough?

Jessica measured Nathan's breathing before he started running, and afterwards. Before running it was 20 breaths a minute. After running it was 35 breaths a minute. Jessica thought about it. Jessica decided that running makes people breathe faster.

Now Jessica was on the right track. If all the other people also breathed faster after exercise she would know her results were really reliable. She needed more results.

Out of breath
The feeling you get that makes you want to breathe faster.

Reliable
Results that you can trust.

Test your learning

On track

1 Ali was playing tennis. He was working really hard!

(a) How will Ali's breathing change while he is playing?

(b) How will the change in breathing help his muscles?

(c) What other changes to his body will he notice while he is working so hard?

Aiming higher

2 Nathan measured a few people's breathing and his own before they played tennis and then again afterwards.

	Breaths per minute before exercise	Breaths per minute after exercise
Nathan	20	35
Jim	22	24
Peter	18	34
Parminder	21	36
Jason	20	38

(a) What do the results show about the effects of exercise on the rate of breathing?

(b) Nathan thought Jim was not working very hard. What made him think that?

(c) Explain why it is a good idea to test a few people.

How well am I doing?

On track

I can describe the changes that happen to us when we exercise.

Aiming higher

I can understand why I need to test a few people in every experiment.

6 What different habitats are there?

- **There are many different kinds of habitat.**
- **Every habitat has its own special group of animals living there.**

There are many different kinds of places where animals and plants can live. All of those different places to live are called **habitats**. Each habitat has its own set of animals and plants who find everything they need there.

What are some habitats?

The plains of Africa

The Arctic ice

Under the sea

A forest

How are animals adapted to their habitat?

A duck's body is just right to live in a pond.

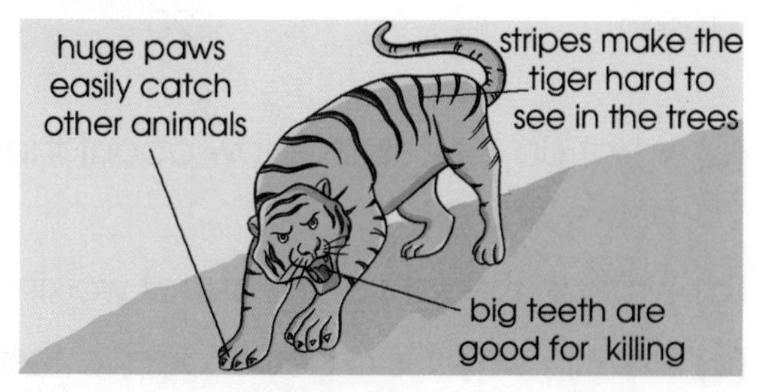

Tigers are best suited to the jungle.

Habitat

The place where animals and plants live.

Adapted

To be specially built to live in a certain place.

Test your learning

On track

1 Here are four habitats.

plains of Africa	Arctic ice	forest	Atlantic Ocean

(a) Copy this table. Use the pictures on the opposite page to describe the habitat. The first one is done for you.

Habitat	Main features
plains of Africa	hot and dry without much shelter/ mostly grassland

Aiming higher

2 The polar bear is adapted to live in the cold Arctic lands around the North Pole.

(a) Why do you think it has such big paws?

(b) How is the polar bear adapted to live in the very cold Arctic?

(c) From this list choose two other animals that also live in the Arctic.

seal	lion	kangaroo	reindeer

How well am I doing?

On track

I can name different habitats.

Aiming higher

I can name some animals that live in different habitats.

7 Where do animals prefer to live?

- Animals choose the right place to live.
- You need to study a few creatures every time to get a reliable result.

How do animals find the right place to live? They always seem to end up in the right sort of place so they must have some way of choosing. Of course we can't ask animals why they do things, so we need to do some experiments instead.

How do woodlice end up underneath logs?

A choice chamber – the woodlice can go in any side they want.

Do woodlice prefer light places or dark places?

Luke and Leia tried this out by covering one side of a choice chamber with a card. How many woodlice would end up on either side after ten minutes?

Why do we need to test a lot of woodlice?

Leia only had three woodlice.

Light side	Dark side
1 woodlouse	2 woodlice

Most woodlice choose the dark, but if just one of them swapped sides you could get the opposite conclusion!

Luke had 30 woodlice.

Light side	Dark side
10 woodlice	20 woodlice

Luke can say, "Most woodlice turn to the dark side". If one or two "change their minds", it will not matter.

If you use a large number of animals you can be sure of your conclusion, even if one or two results are not what you expected.

Choice chamber

Equipment that lets you see what conditions animals prefer.

Conclusion

What your experiment has proved.

Test your learning

On track

1 Leopard class thought that woodlice would prefer damp soil to dry soil. They decided to test their idea.

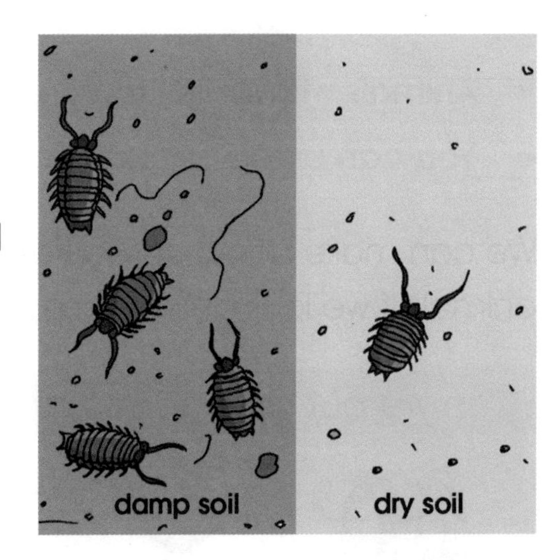

They put some soil in a shoe box. At one end the soil was dry and at the other end it was damp. They put five woodlice in the middle and put the lid on to make the box dark.

After 30 minutes they came back. This is where the woodlice were.

(a) Show the results in the form of a table.

	Damp soil	Dry soil
Number of woodlice		

(b) What would be Leopard class's best conclusion?

- Woodlice prefer dark places.
- Woodlice prefer damp places.
- Woodlice don't mind whether the soil is damp or dry.

Aiming higher

2 Jessica thought about the experiment. She knew she could make a better one.

(a) Jessica wanted to try the same experiment, but use 50 woodlice. Why was that a good idea?

(b) She was glad she had made sure both sides were in the dark by putting a lid on. Why was that a good idea?

How well am I doing?

On track

I can do experiments to see how animals choose where to live.

Aiming higher

I can make my results reliable by testing a lot of animals.

8 How can you identify plants and animals?

- **Animals with similar features can be put into groups.**
- **You can use a key to find out the names of plants and animals.**

We can make books called **keys** that tell us the names of plants and animals if we look at their features and answer a few simple questions.

Can we put animals into groups?

Indian water buffalo

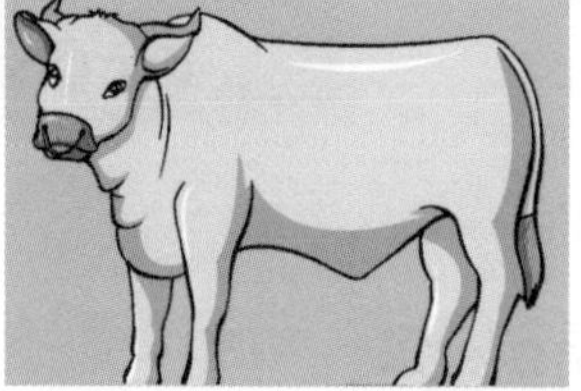

British farm bull

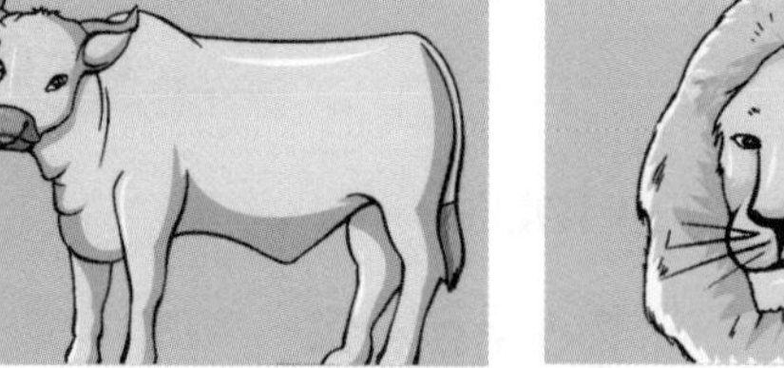

African lion

South American jaguar

These grass-eaters come from different countries. They are big and strong, with horns.

These big cats share the same features. They are hunters from different countries.

If we don't know the name of a plant or animal, how can we find it out?

If we have a key, we can soon find the names.

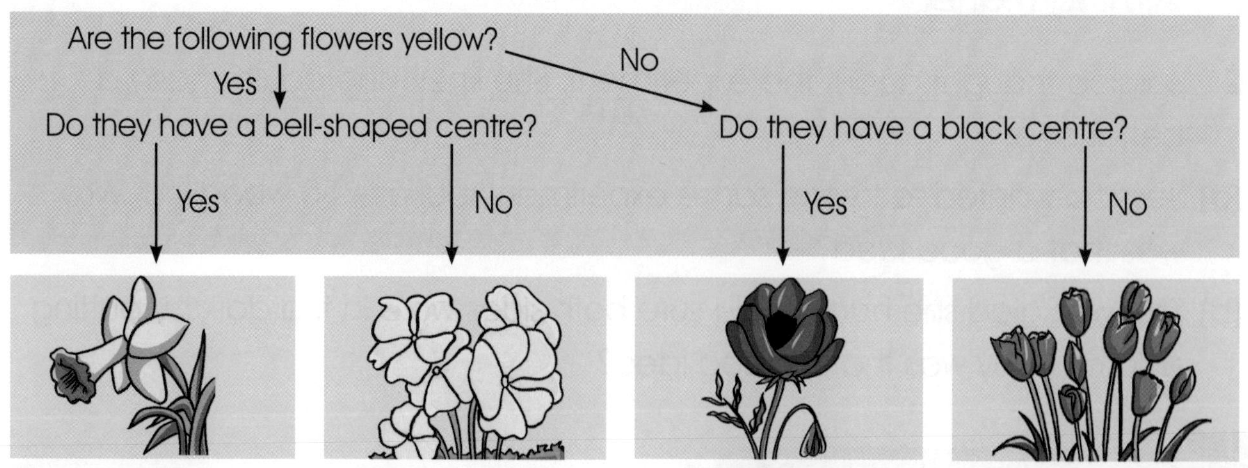

Key

A way of finding out the names of plants or animals.

Features

Important ways of recognising an animal, such as claws or horns.

Test your learning

On track

1

mouse

rat

rabbit

hare

(a) Name two features that would make you put the mouse and the rat into the same group.

(b) Rabbits and hares are in the same group, but they are not exactly the same as each other. Name a feature that lets you tell them apart.

Aiming higher

2 Jessica was collecting fruits and seeds.
This is one she found.

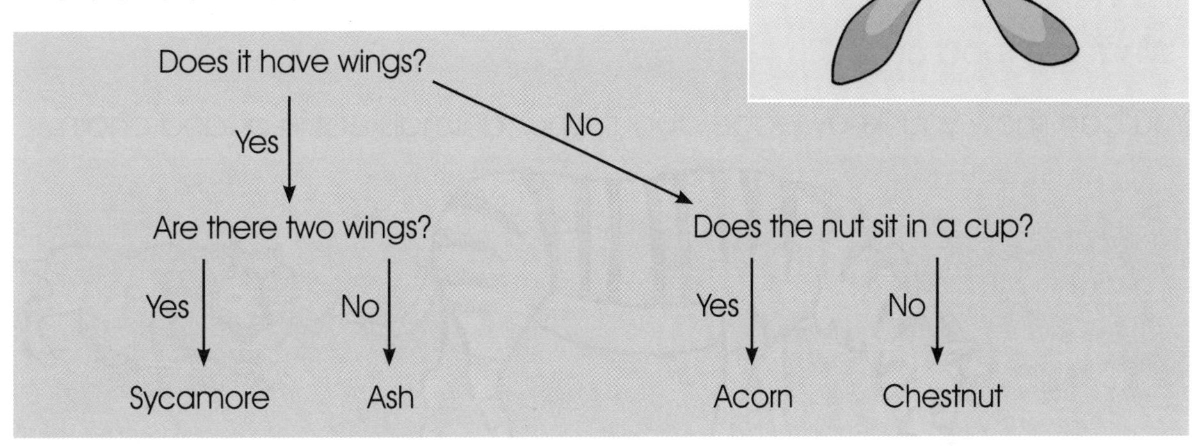

(a) What is the name of the one she found?

(b) Which fruit does not have any wings or a cup to hold the nut?

How well am I doing?

On track

I can put some animals and plants into their groups.

Aiming higher

I can use a key to find the names of animals and plants.

9 What do different animals eat?

- Some animals eat plants, and some eat other animals.
- You can show what animals eat by making a food chain.

Some animals, like foxes, only eat meat. Others, like rabbits, only eat grass and other green plants. The meat-eaters have to go hunting to catch other animals to eat. The plant-eaters try to keep out of the way of the hunters!

What are predators and what are prey?

The fox is a **predator**. That means he is a hunter. He catches and eats rabbits.

The blackbird eats worms, so he is a **predator** just like the fox.

The rabbit eats grass and other plants. Rabbits are the **prey** of the fox – he eats them.

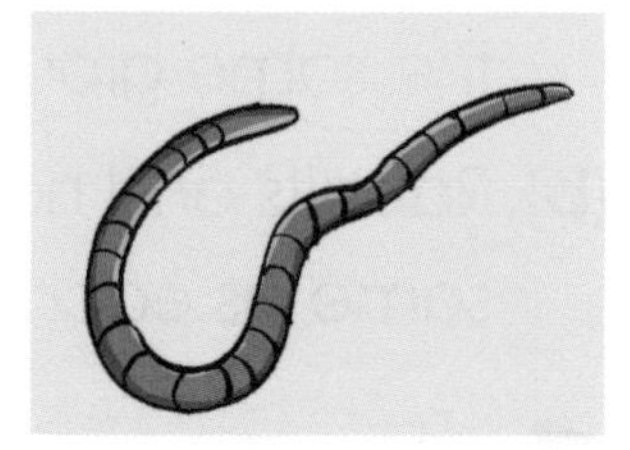

Worms are the blackbird's **prey**. Worms eat dead leaves.

What is a food chain?

You can show your knowledge about what animals eat in a food chain.

grass ⟶ zebra ⟶ lion

The grass makes the food in the first place. Then the zebra eats the grass, and finally the lion eats the zebra. The food is being passed along the chain.

Producer

"Produce" means "make". Green plants produce the food that starts every food chain.

Consumer

"Consume" means "eat". Zebras and lions are both consumers.

Test your learning

On track

1 These animals like to eat different things.

wolf

sheep

cat

chicken

horse

eagle

(a) Copy this table and fill it in to show what the different animals eat.

Meat-eaters	Plant-eaters
eagle	

(b) What clue in the picture tells you the eagle is a meat-eater?

Aiming higher

2 Here are a few facts about some animals and what they eat.

owl

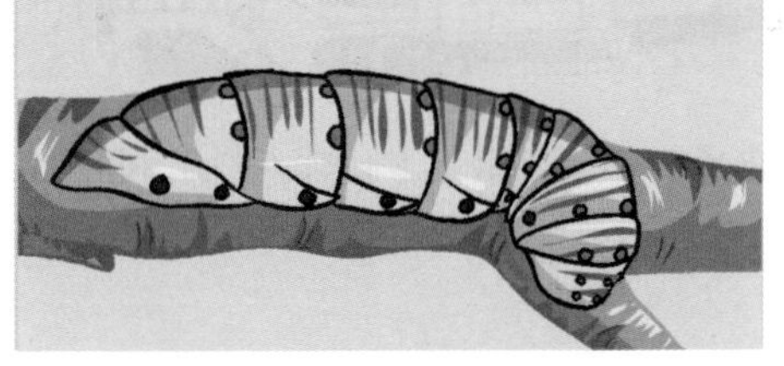
A caterpillar eats lettuce leaves.

A thrush eats caterpillars.

(a) Copy this table and show everything as a food chain.

	→		→		→	

(b) From the food chain above name one **producer** and three **consumers**.

How well am I doing?

On track

I can say that predators eat other animals, which are called their prey.

Aiming higher

I can show what animals eat in a food chain.

10 How can we look after habitats?

- **Habitats are in danger of being spoiled.**
- **People can do lots of things to help look after natural habitats.**

All sorts of things can spoil a habitat. A river might cause a flood and fill up a field with water. All the mice and rabbits and foxes would have to go and live somewhere else. But the main thing spoiling habitats is … us!

Why do people spoil habitats?

There are so many people in the world … and they all need somewhere to live!

Over 7,000,000 people live in London.

Your house is probably on a piece of land that was once a wild habitat.

Only the tree has survived. Everything else has gone to make room for the house.

How can we look after natural habitats?

We need to make sure that some space is left for the animals and plants. You might have a country park near you. The animals and plants can carry on if we just leave them some space.

Mina wrote a letter to Mr Sharma. She asked if the school could have a wildflower garden in a part of the school field.

Conservation

Keeping wild places in their natural state.

Country park

A place like a wood or a lake that you can visit to see animals and plants.

Test your learning

On track

Owls eat mice.

1 More and more people are moving into the town where Mr Sharma's school is. Lots of new houses are being built for the people to live in.

(a) Why will building new homes in the town make it harder for owls to survive there?

(b) Out in the countryside the farmers are getting rid of their hedges to make their fields bigger. Why does that make it harder for owls to live?

Aiming higher

2 Mr Sharma read Mina's letter and decided to let part of the school field go wild. It did not get mowed any more, and wild flowers and little bushes started to grow in the long grass. Some of the children saw rabbits there. Mina, who lives near the school, thought she saw a fox in the school field one evening.

(a) How did not mowing the grass help the rabbits?

(b) Why did the fox start to visit the school field?

How well am I doing?

On track

I can describe how wild habitats are sometimes spoilt by people.

Aiming higher

I can explain how we can help to look after wild habitats.

11 How is temperature measured?

- **The temperature of an object tells us how hot or cold it is.**
- **You can measure the temperature with a thermometer.**

Is it cold outside today? Do you sometimes get hot when you are running around? How hot do you like your food? Do you sometimes feel the swimming pool is too cold? We can measure temperatures to be sure they are just right.

Is it hot, or is it cold?

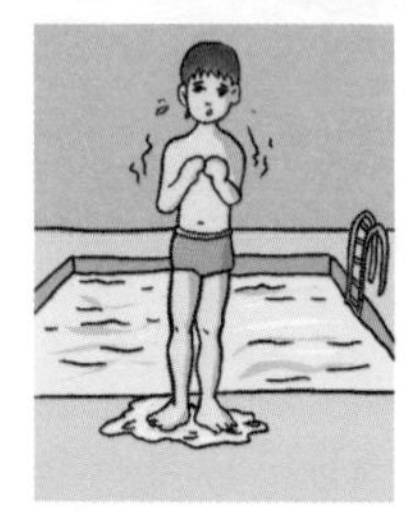

Brrr! It's cold when you get out of the water!

Is the lolly even colder?

This tea is nice and hot.

Is the desert hotter than the tea, or colder?

You can use the words "hot" and "cold" to describe **temperatures** but that is not very accurate or scientific. We need a better way.

How can we tell exactly how hot things are?

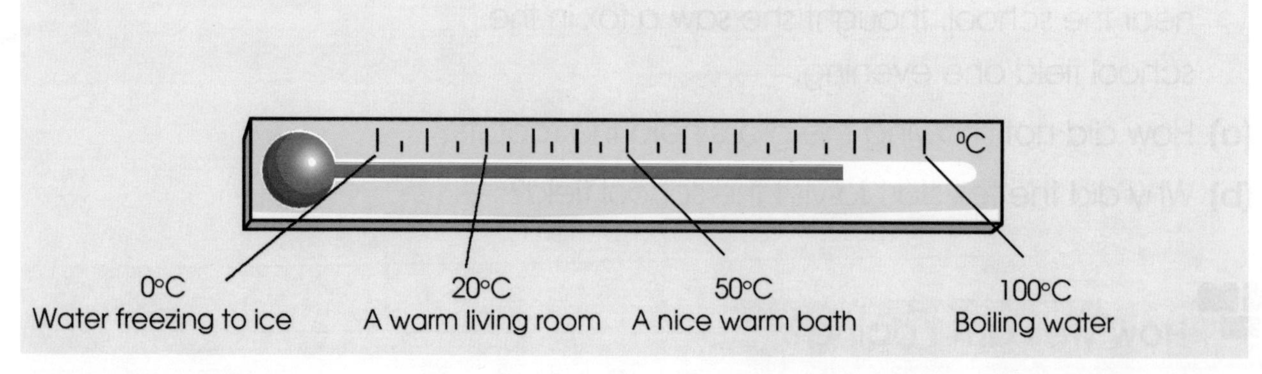

A **thermometer** gives us the temperature in degrees Celsius, which are written °C. Your body temperature is 37°C.

Temperature

How hot or cold something is.

Celsius

The scientist who divided the temperatures between freezing and boiling into 100 degrees.

Test your learning

On track

1 Mina thought about all the different types of liquid she saw during the day.

(a) Copy the table and fill in the right words from the list.

cold	**iced drink**
cool	**water from kettle**
warm	**water for washing**
hot	**swimming pool water**

(b) What did Mina need to measure to find out which liquid is the hottest?

Aiming higher

2

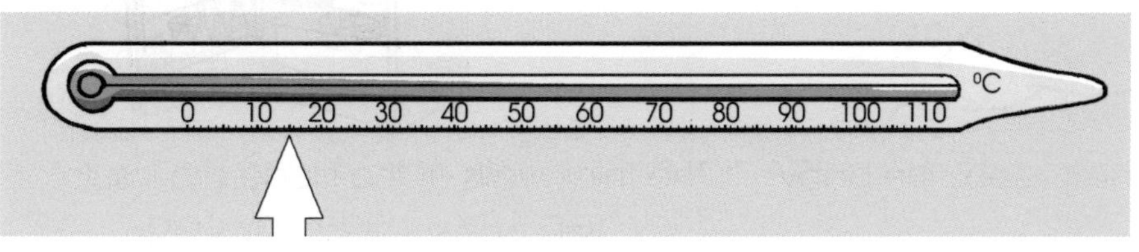

(a) What temperature is the arrow pointing at?

(b) Put these temperatures in the right place in the table.

0°C	**a frosty morning in winter**
18°C	**boiling water**
25°C	**a hot summer day**
100°C	**a drink of tap water**

How well am I doing?

On track

I know that hot things have high temperatures and cold things have low temperatures.

Aiming higher

I can measure the temperature in °C with a thermometer.

12 What keeps things hot or cold?

- Insulators keep hot things hot and cold things cold.
- Things cool down or warm up to be the same as their surroundings.

How can you stop a lolly melting? How can you keep your chips hot? The same answer will do for both jobs. Wrapping them up in an **insulator** (like a fleece, for example) could keep the chips hot and also keep the lolly cold.

What do insulators do?

Keeping hot things hot

The duvet is an insulator. It keeps the baby nice and warm!

Keeping cold things cold

The thick walls of the fridge are insulators. They help things inside stay cold.

How do insulators work?

Things put in the same room will end up at the same temperature.

The hot tea and the cold drink will soon be at 20°C, room temperature. Heat from the tea escapes into the room; heat from the room warms up the iced drink.

Insulators slow that down. Things keep their own temperature for longer.

The heat can't get in or out of this insulated jug. It keeps tea hot, or an iced drink cold!

Insulator

Any material that stops heat going through it. Plastic and wood are insulators.

Conductor

Any material that allows heat to go through it. Metals are conductors.

Test your learning

On track

1 Ali put some ice lollies into two jam jars. He wrapped up one jar with cloth.

A jam jar with a lolly inside

A jam jar with a lolly inside, wrapped up with cloth

After 90 minutes the lolly in the jar without the cloth wrapping had melted.

(a) How long would it take the lolly in the wrapped-up jar to melt?

less than 90 minutes | **90 minutes** | **more than 90 minutes**

(b) What is the name for a wrapping that keeps cold things cold?

insulator | **conductor** | **protractor**

Aiming higher

2 At home, Ali had an iced drink. Its temperature was 5°C. His mum had a cup of tea that was 60°C. They left them in the kitchen, which was 20°C, and forgot to drink them!

An hour later they found their drinks.

(a) What temperature would the drinks be when they found them? Pick the right temperature for each one.

Ali's drink	5°C	20°C	60°C
Mum's drink	5°C	20°C	60°C

(b) How would an insulated cup have helped keep the drinks at the right temperature?

How well am I doing?

On track

I can say that insulating something stops its temperature from changing.

Aiming higher

I can say that objects get warmer or colder to match the surroundings.

13 What is the best insulator?

- You can do a fair test to find the best insulator.
- You can put your results down clearly in a table and graph.

Your clothes keep you warm, so we know they are insulators. Fur and feathers keep animals and birds warm, so they must be insulators too. Which are best?

Which is the best insulator to keep cold things cold?

Jam jar	Wrapping	Time to melt
1	none	10 minutes
2	cotton wool	20 minutes
3	fleece	30 minutes

Conclusion: Fleece was the best insulator.

Jessica had three jars. She put a few ice cubes into each jar. She wrapped up two of the jars in different insulators. She then timed how long it took the cubes to melt.

Was the test fair?

Jessica kept two things the same each time to make the test fair.

- The insulators were the same thickness.
- The jars were at the same temperature.

Can we use a graph to see our results clearly?

This time Jessica had some warm water in her three jars.

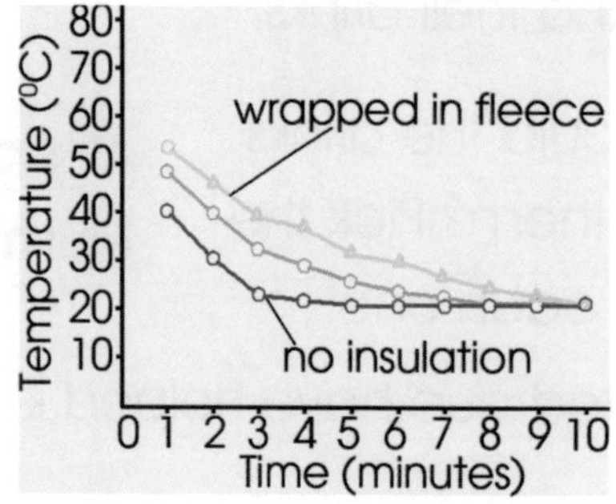

The warm water without any insulation cooled down to room temperature first.

The slowest to cool down was the beaker wrapped in fleece!

Fair test

Keeping everything the same for each test, except for the variable that is being tested.

Table

A way of keeping figures neat by putting them in boxes drawn with a ruler.

Test your learning

On track

1 Nathan wanted to know if cotton wool would insulate the beaker and keep the water warm. He wrapped up one beaker in cotton wool and took the temperature every five minutes.

A beaker of warm water

A beaker of warm water wrapped in cotton wool

To make his test fair he decided to keep as many things as he could the same for each beaker. They both started off at the same temperature, for example.

(a) Name three other things he could have kept the same to make his test fair.

(b) Why should he have tested the two beakers at the same time?

Aiming higher

2 Here are his results.

Beaker X	
Time	**Temperature**
0 minutes	60°C
5 minutes	40°C
10 minutes	25°C
15 minutes	22°C
20 minutes	20°C

Beaker Y	
Time	**Temperature**
0 minutes	60°C
5 minutes	30°C
10 minutes	21°C
15 minutes	20°C
20 minutes	20°C

(a) Which beaker, X or Y, cooled down fastest?

(b) Which beaker, X or Y, was the insulated one?

How well am I doing?

On track

I can make a test fair by changing only one thing at a time.

Aiming higher

I can show my results properly in a table.

14 How are conductors and insulators useful?

- We often need to keep things warm (or cold) using insulators.
- Metals conduct electricity as well as heat.

Now you know what insulators are, you can find them everywhere in your house. Your whole house is a great big insulator, keeping you warm in the winter. Your clothes do the same job. Look in the kitchen – there are quite a few insulators to find there.

How do we use insulators to keep things warm or cold?

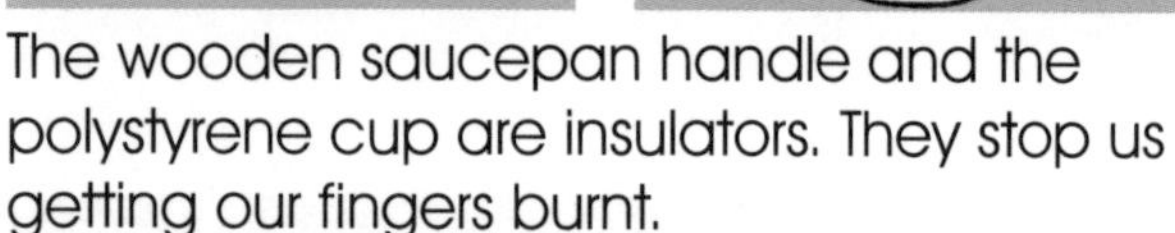

The wooden saucepan handle and the polystyrene cup are insulators. They stop us getting our fingers burnt.

Padded ski clothes and thick boots keep our heat inside.

What materials let heat and electricity through easily?

This metal wok cooks the vegetables really well. Metals are very good **conductors** of heat.

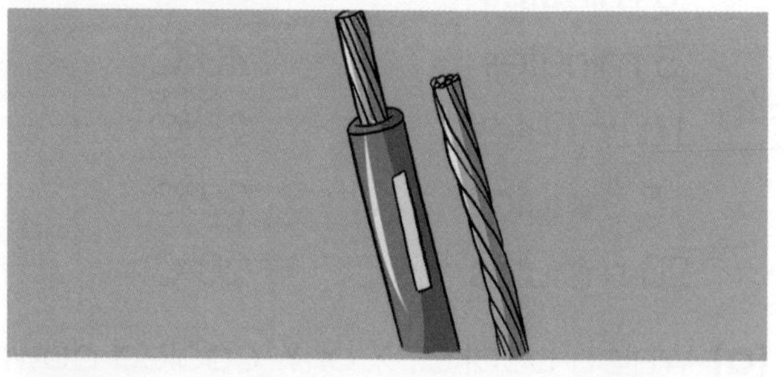

Metals (such as copper) are also good **conductors** of electricity. The insulating plastic around the copper wire keeps us safe!

Thermal conductor

A material that lets heat pass through easily.

Electrical conductor

A material that lets electricity pass through easily.

Science Study Guide: Year 4

Answer Booklet

<table>
<tr><th>Unit</th><th></th><th>On track</th><th></th><th>Aiming higher</th></tr>
<tr><td>1 What animals have skeletons?</td><td>1 (a)

(b)</td><td>(1) skeleton
(2) vertebrate
(3) invertebrate
<table><tr><th>Vertebrates</th><th>Invertebrates</th></tr><tr><td>cow</td><td>snail</td></tr><tr><td>horse</td><td>octopus</td></tr><tr><td>eagle</td><td>slug</td></tr></table></td><td>2 (a)

(b)</td><td>The frog's legs are much longer, and its feet are also very big.
The long legs help it jump a long distance. The big feet help it to swim.</td></tr>
<tr><td>2 What are bones like?</td><td>1 (a)
(b)</td><td>Bone C
The horse is a big animal and its bones carry a lot of weight, so the bones need to be very strong and thick.</td><td>2 (a)</td><td>Gorillas eat very (1) tough food. They need very (2) strong jaw muscles, so they have a big (3) ridge on their heads for the (4) muscles to hold onto.</td></tr>
<tr><td>3 How fast does your skeleton grow?</td><td>1 (a)
(b)
(c)</td><td>Ewan
Aidan
45 cm</td><td>2 (a)</td><td>Experiment 1 and prediction 3
Experiment 2 and prediction 2
Experiment 3 and prediction 1</td></tr>
<tr><td>4 How do muscles move bones?</td><td>1 (a)
(b)</td><td>muscles
pulling</td><td>2 (a)

(b)</td><td>• Back muscles pull (contract).
• Tummy muscles stretch (relax).
The tummy muscles pull (contract) and the back muscles relax (stretch).</td></tr>
<tr><td>5 How do muscles help you exercise?</td><td>1 (a)
(b)

(c)</td><td>He will breathe faster.
It will give his muscles more oxygen.
He will sweat and feel tired.</td><td>2 (a)
(b)

(c)</td><td>Exercise makes you breathe faster.
There is little difference between how many breaths Jim takes before and after exercise.
To make your results more accurate and reliable.</td></tr>
<tr><td>6 What different habitats are there?</td><td>1 (a)</td><td><table><tr><th>Habitat</th><th>Main features</th></tr><tr><td>Arctic ice</td><td>very cold/little plant growth</td></tr><tr><td>Forest</td><td>wide variety of plants/lots of shelter</td></tr><tr><td>Atlantic ocean</td><td>salt water</td></tr></table></td><td>2 (a)

(b)

(c)</td><td>To provide grip/to help kill seals/to swim better/to avoid sinking into the snow.
Its thick fur and layers of fat keep it warm. It is white (camouflage).
Seal and reindeer</td></tr>
<tr><td>7 Where do animals prefer to live?</td><td>1 (a)

(b)</td><td><table><tr><th></th><th>Damp soil</th><th>Dry soil</th></tr><tr><td>Number of woodlice</td><td>4</td><td>1</td></tr></table>Woodlice prefer damp places.</td><td>2 (a)

(b)</td><td>The results will be better./The conclusion will be more reliable.
It helped make the tests fair.</td></tr>
<tr><td>8 How can you identify plants and animals?</td><td>1 (a)

(b)</td><td>They both have short ears. They both have pointed snouts.
Hares are generally larger./Hares have longer hind legs./Hares have longer ears.</td><td>2 (a)
(b)</td><td>Sycamore seeds
Chestnut</td></tr>
</table>

<table>
<tr><th>Unit</th><th></th><th>On track</th><th></th><th>Aiming higher</th></tr>
<tr><td>9 What do different animals eat?</td><td>1 (a)

(b)</td><td><table><tr><th>Meat-eaters</th><th>Plant-eaters</th></tr><tr><td>wolf</td><td>sheep</td></tr><tr><td>cat</td><td>chicken</td></tr><tr><td></td><td>horse</td></tr></table>Its beak is built to rip and tear.</td><td>2 (a)

(b)</td><td>Lettuce ⟶ Caterpillar ⟶
Thrush ⟶ Owl
Producer: lettuce leaves
Consumers: caterpillar, thrush, owl</td></tr>
<tr><td>10 How can we look after habitats?</td><td>1 (a)

(b)</td><td>Fewer places to nest/fewer small creatures to hunt
Their food (mice, etc.) lives in the hedgerows.</td><td>2 (a)
(b)</td><td>More grass for rabbits to eat.
Foxes visit to hunt rabbits.</td></tr>
<tr><td>11 How is temperature measured?</td><td>1 (a)

(b)</td><td><table><tr><td>iced drink</td><td>cold</td></tr><tr><td>water from kettle</td><td>hot</td></tr><tr><td>water for washing</td><td>warm</td></tr><tr><td>swimming pool water</td><td>cool</td></tr></table>The temperature</td><td>2 (a)
(b)</td><td>15°C<table><tr><td>A frosty morning in winter</td><td>0°C</td></tr><tr><td>Boiling water</td><td>100°C</td></tr><tr><td>A hot summer day</td><td>25°C</td></tr><tr><td>A drink of tap water</td><td>18°C</td></tr></table></td></tr>
<tr><td>12 What keeps things hot or cold?</td><td>1 (a)
(b)</td><td>120 mins
Insulator</td><td>2 (a)
(b)</td><td>Ali's drink 20°C/Mum's drink 20°C
It would have stopped heat getting in or out of the cups.</td></tr>
<tr><td>13 What is the best insulator?</td><td>1 (a)

(b)</td><td>Use the same amount of water. Keep the temperature of the jar at the start the same. Keep the jars in the same place in the room.
To make a fair comparison./To make sure the air around them is at the same temperature.</td><td>2 (a)
(b)</td><td>Beaker Y
Beaker X</td></tr>
<tr><td>14 How are conductors and insulators useful?</td><td>1 (a)

(b)</td><td>Plastic is an insulating material and stops heat getting to your hand.
Wooden spoon, plastic cup, wooden saucepan handle</td><td>2 (a)</td><td>1 a thermal conductor
2 an electrical conductor
3 an electrical insulator</td></tr>
<tr><td>15 How are solids and liquids different?</td><td>1 (a)

(b)</td><td>Solids: ice, chocolate, wood, iron. Liquids: petrol, milk, blood.
Water takes the shape of the container it is in./The volume of water in each container is the same.</td><td>2 (a)
(b)</td><td>It poured
The individual particles of sand are hard. They keep their shape and cannot be squashed.</td></tr>
<tr><td>16 What are melting points?</td><td>1 (a)
(b)

(c)
(d)</td><td>Melting
Chocolate has a melting point just below that of Ali's mouth.
Both melted, the lolly much faster.
0°C</td><td>2 (a)

(b)</td><td>Metal spoon and gold ring: Both are made of a metal./These solids have the highest melting points.
Butter and chocolate.</td></tr>
<tr><td>17 Can mixtures be separated?</td><td>1 (a)
(b)</td><td>Rice and salt
Stuffing and mixed vegetables</td><td>2 (a)

(b)</td><td><table><tr><th>Equipment</th><th>Properties</th></tr><tr><td>1 Magnet</td><td>Iron is magnetic, salt is not.</td></tr><tr><td>2 Garden sieve</td><td>Soil particles are much smaller.</td></tr><tr><td>3 Water</td><td>Salt dissolves in water, sand does not.</td></tr><tr><td>4 Kitchen sieve</td><td>Flour particles are smaller.</td></tr></table>First use a garden sieve to sieve out the pebbles. Then add water – the salt dissolves leaving sand behind. Filter off the sand. Finally, heat the salt water mixture to get back the salt.</td></tr>
</table>

<table>
<tr><th>Unit</th><th></th><th>On track</th><th></th><th>Aiming higher</th></tr>
<tr><td>18 What happens when you mix solids and liquids?</td><td>1 (a)
(b)

(c)</td><td>Liquids: water and vinegar.
Solids: sand, coffee and bicarbonate of soda.
A</td><td>2 (a)

(b)

(c)</td><td>Salt: It seems to disappear into the water.
Plaster of Paris: a new material is made.
Glass beads: nothing seems to happen – they just sink.</td></tr>
<tr><td>19 How can you separate solids from liquids?</td><td>1 (a)</td><td>Kitchen colander – 1
Blotting paper – 2
Muslin – 3</td><td>2 (a)

(b)</td><td>The sieve removed the stones but the water and sand went through.
Sand and stones stayed on the filter paper, water passed through.</td></tr>
<tr><td>20 What are the stages in a test?</td><td>1 (a)</td><td>1 Think of a question to test.
2 Make a prediction.
3 Decide how to do the test.
4 Carry out the test.
5 Make observations.
6 Make sense of the results.
7 See if the results match the prediction or not.</td><td>2 (a)

(b)

(c)

(d)</td><td>2 Fact: I know that sugar dissolves in water.
1 Question to test: Can you get sugar back from a sugary solution by filtering?
4 Prediction: It will not be possible to separate sugar from sugary water.
3 Observation: All the sugar solution goes through the filter paper.</td></tr>
<tr><td>21 How are forces measured?</td><td>1 (a)
(b)
(c)</td><td>5 N
8 N
Newton meter/spring balance</td><td>2 (a)
(b)</td><td>The bucket
newton</td></tr>
<tr><td>22 Can friction be useful?</td><td>1 (a)

(b)</td><td>High friction: sandpaper and carpet.
Low friction: ice and glass.
Other examples of high friction: road surface, table cloth, sole of a shoe, bike tyre, etc.</td><td>2 (a)

(b)</td><td>High friction is helpful in holding your bicycle handlebars, tying your shoelaces and walking.
Low friction is helpful in swimming, a car engine working smoothly, roller skating, a fighter plane flying fast and pulling a drawer out of a desk.
Making the surfaces smooth or wet or lubricating them.</td></tr>
<tr><td>23 How do you test for friction?</td><td>1 (a)

(b)</td><td>A stopwatch and a tape measure. He is not measuring time or distance.
The force (in newtons) needed to make the trainer start moving.</td><td>2 (a)

(b)
(c)</td><td>1 Ali kept the trainer the same.
2 He changed the surface.
3 He would measure the force needed to make the trainer start to move.
Friction
Newtons</td></tr>
<tr><td>24 How do we show results clearly?</td><td>1 (a)
(b)
(c)</td><td>Material A
Materials C and D
<table><tr><th>Material</th><th>Friction (N)</th></tr><tr><td>A</td><td>10</td></tr><tr><td>B</td><td>15</td></tr><tr><td>C</td><td>20</td></tr><tr><td>D</td><td>20</td></tr><tr><td>E</td><td>30</td></tr></table></td><td>2 (a)

(b)</td><td>The smoother the material the lower the friction.
That for material I: it is rougher than H but produces lower friction.</td></tr>
</table>

<table>
<tr><th>Unit</th><th></th><th>On track</th><th></th><th>Aiming higher</th></tr>
<tr><td>25 What is water resistance?</td><td>1 (a)
(b)</td><td>Water resistance – a kind of friction.
The lower the water resistance the easier the ship will go through water./To reduce running costs.</td><td>2 (a)

(b)</td><td>The plasticine was the same weight every time./The cylinder was the same every time.
Yes</td></tr>
<tr><td>26 Why do some electrical circuits not work?</td><td>1 (a)
(b)
(c)</td><td>Provide power/make electricity.
Connect the cells correctly.
A and C</td><td>2 (a)

(b)</td><td>The switch might be open, part of the circuit contains an insulating material, there is a gap in the circuit. Cells could be the wrong way round.
Circuit drawn correctly.</td></tr>
<tr><td>27 Which materials let electricity pass through?</td><td>1 (a)
(b)</td><td>The metal core.
To stop electricity reaching you.</td><td>2 (a)

(b)</td><td>Conductors: metal key, ring pull, gold ring.
Insulators: feather, stone.
Electrical conductors: any material made of metal.
Electrical insulators: anything made out of plastic or another non-metal.</td></tr>
<tr><td>28 How do switches work?</td><td>1 (a)

(b)</td><td>Any two of: a camera/microwave oven/torch/iPod/mobile phone.
To save power/to stop the battery running out.</td><td>2 (a)
(b)
(c)</td><td>Nothing
The bulb will light.
A switch when open makes a gap in the circuit so no electricity flows. Electricity flows when the switch is closed.</td></tr>
<tr><td>29 What affects how brightly a bulb lights up?</td><td>1 (a)

(b)</td><td>Does changing the number of bulbs in a circuit affect how brightly they light up?
<table>
<tr><th></th><th>What she kept the same</th><th>What she changed</th><th>What she observed</th></tr>
<tr><td>Number of bulbs</td><td></td><td>✓</td><td></td></tr>
<tr><td>Type of bulbs</td><td>✓</td><td></td><td></td></tr>
<tr><td>Number of cells</td><td>✓</td><td></td><td></td></tr>
<tr><td>Brightness of bulb(s)</td><td></td><td></td><td>✓</td></tr>
</table></td><td>2 (a)

(b)

(c)</td><td>
<table>
<tr><th></th><th>What she kept the same</th><th>What she changed</th><th>What she observed</th></tr>
<tr><td>Number of bulbs</td><td>✓</td><td></td><td></td></tr>
<tr><td>Type of bulbs</td><td>✓</td><td></td><td></td></tr>
<tr><td>Number of cells</td><td></td><td>✓</td><td></td></tr>
<tr><td>Brightness of bulb(s)</td><td></td><td></td><td>✓</td></tr>
</table>
Suitable circuits drawn using the correct symbols or drawings.
Circuits correctly labelled.</td></tr>
</table>

Design: Clive Sutherland

Test your learning

On track

1 This is Mr Sharma's new kettle. He likes it because it is made of shiny metal with a plastic handle.

(a) Explain why it is a good idea to have a plastic handle on a kettle.

(b) Which of these objects are made of insulators, to stop you getting burnt?

wooden spoon **plastic cup** **glass windows**

metal spoon **metal frying pan** **wooden saucepan handle**

Aiming higher

2 Copper metal is used in saucepan bottoms because it lets the heat through from the cooker flame really well. Food cooks quickly in copper saucepans. Mina noticed that electric wires are also made of copper, and that they are always wrapped up in plastic.

(a) Fill in the sentences with the descriptions in the box.

an electrical conductor	an electrical insulator	a thermal conductor

1 Copper lets heat through easily because it is ________________

2 Wires are made of copper because it is ________________

3 Plastic wrapping on wires stops you getting a shock because it is

____

How well am I doing?

On track

I can spot conductors and insulators being used in my home.

Aiming higher

I can explain that metals conduct heat and electricity well.

15 How are solids and liquids different?

- **Solids and liquids have different properties.**
- **Some solids seem to be a bit like a liquid.**

Most materials are either **solids** or **liquids** at room temperature. Solids like iron keep their shape. Liquids like water change shape and can be poured. Solids with very small particles appear to pour but they are still in fact solids.

How are solids and liquids different?

Solids:

- are hard and are difficult to compress
- keep their shape when you move them.

Most liquids:

- pour and are runny
- take the shape of their containers.

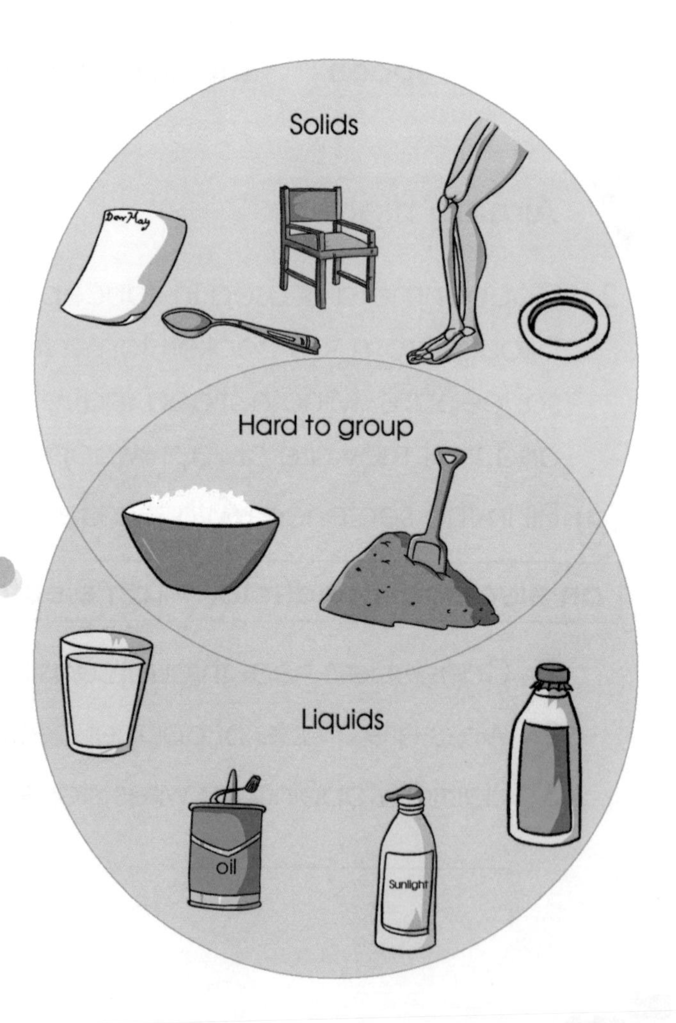

Why are some materials hard to group?

Grains of rice are hard. This makes you think it is a solid. However, you can liquidise and pour the grains into a bottle just like a liquid.

Most scientists agree rice is a solid because, although it pours, each grain is hard.

Group

A collection of things which are similar.

Compress

To squeeze and compact together.

Test your learning

On track

1 Here are some everyday solids and liquids.

petrol **ice** **milk** **chocolate** **wood** **blood** **iron**

(a) Sort the materials into two groups. Make one list of the solids and one of the liquids.

Mina poured 100 cm^3 of water into four different-shaped containers.

(b) Which of these statements are true?

- Solids can be poured.
- Water takes the shape of the container it is in.
- Water is a solid.
- The volume of water in each container is the same.

Aiming higher

2 Mina was on the beach. She tipped some sand from her spade into her bucket.

(a) What could Mina see that made her think sand might be a liquid?

(b) What is it about sand that makes us decide it is a solid?

How well am I doing?

On track

I can describe how solids and liquids are different.

Aiming higher

I can say why some materials are difficult to group.

16 What are melting points?

- **Solids change into liquids at a temperature called the melting point.**
- **Different materials have different melting points.**

Solids change into liquids when heated. This process is called melting. Some solids melt at very low temperatures. Others, such as metals, melt at very high temperatures. Liquids freeze into solids when they are cooled.

What happens at melting points?

Chocolate is usually solid but if you warm it up it will melt to a liquid.

Chocolate is made to melt just above 36°C. This means it melts in your mouth.

How different are melting points?

Metals such as gold melt at high temperatures. Gold melts into a liquid at over 1000°C.

Candle wax melts at around 150°C. A hot flame will melt it.

Butter melts between 30°C–35°C. On most days in Britain it is solid, but it will melt on a very hot day.

Solid water is called ice. Ice changes to liquid water when it is heated above 0°C. It freezes to ice when cooled below 0°C.

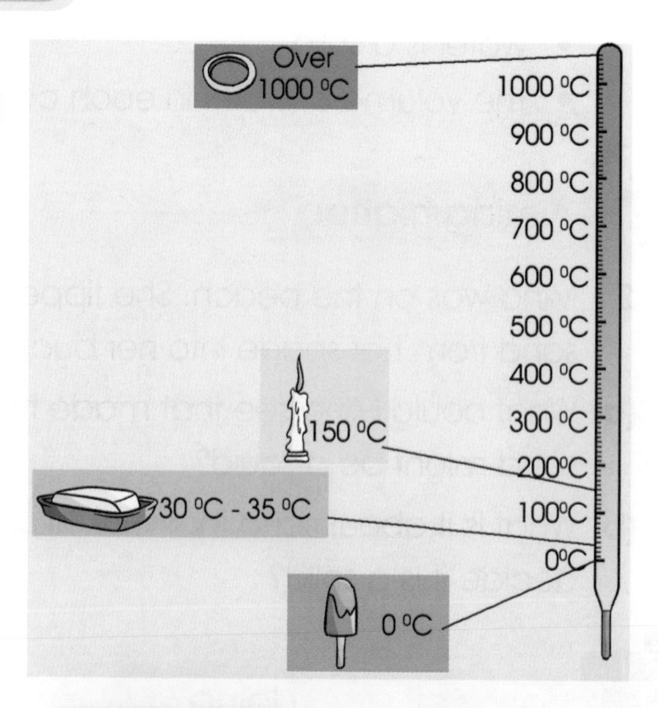

Melting point

The temperature at which a solid changes into its liquid.

Freezing point

The temperature at which a liquid changes into its solid.

Test your learning

On track

1 Ali had an ice lolly and some chocolate to eat. It was 30°C outside and very warm.

(a) What is the name given to the process when Ali's lolly and chocolate change from a solid into a liquid?

(b) Ali ate a piece of chocolate. Explain why it melted in his mouth.

(c) Ali left the lolly and chocolate on the table. What happened to them?

(d) Ali put his lolly into a freezer. What should the temperature be so that it stays solid?

Aiming higher

2 Ali had four different materials. He wondered at what temperature they would melt.

Butter	Iron	Chocolate	Gold

(a) Which two materials have the highest melting points? Explain your answer.

(b) Which materials would melt on a hot day?

How well am I doing?

On track

I can explain what the words "melting point" mean.

Aiming higher

Name some materials that melt at very high temperatures.

17 Can mixtures be separated?

- **Mixtures of solids contain small pieces of different materials jumbled up.**
- **Mixtures can be separated if you have the right equipment.**

Pure solids contain just one kind of "stuff", or particles in them. If you mix two or more pure solids together you make a **mixture**. This is easy. A harder job is to take a mixture and, using the correct equipment, get back the pure solids.

What is a mixture?

This is a mixture of peas and sweetcorn. You can see what it is because the pieces are quite big. If sand and salt are mixed together it is quite hard to see the difference between the two – but they are both there.

How can a sieve separate a mixture?

Mr Sharma asked his class: "How would you separate this mixture of sand, rice and dried peas?"

Ali answered: "Rice, sand and dried peas are all different sizes. Let's use some sieves!"

Look what happens! The big peas are trapped, but the smaller rice and sand grains pass through this sieve with big holes.

The sieve with smaller holes traps the rice, but lets the small sand grains pass through into the bowl.

Mixture

A substance which contains two or more materials not joined together.

Sieve

A container with a fine wire mesh used for straining or separating.

Test your learning

On track

1 Jessica bought some items from the shop.

(a) Which items contain pure materials?

(b) Which items are mixtures of solids?

Aiming higher

2 Jessica had four mixtures she wanted to separate. She had a garden sieve, a kitchen sieve, a magnet and some water to help her.

Mixture	Equipment used	What properties make the materials different?
1 salt and iron	Magnet	Iron is magnetic, salt is not.
2 pebbles and soil		
3 salt and sand		
4 flour and currants		

(a) Copy the table. In the middle column write down the equipment Jessica used to separate each mixture. In the right-hand column write down the properties that make the materials in each mixture different. The first one has been done for you.

(b) Explain how you would separate a mixture of pebbles, salt and sand.

How well am I doing?

On track

I can explain what a mixture is.

Aiming higher

I can select the right equipment to separate a mixture of solids.

18 What happens when you mix solids and liquids?

- **Different changes can happen when solids are added to liquids.**
- **Observations help you find out what's going on.**

Different things happen when solids and liquids are mixed. The solid might dissolve in the liquid. Some mixtures react to form new materials. They might just mix. Observing the mixtures gives you clues about what has happened.

What can you see when solids and liquids are mixed?

Nathan, Ali and Mina mixed materials together. They looked carefully at what happened. Ali organised their observations in a table. They tried to make sense of what they saw.

Sand and water

"The sand sinks to the bottom of the water."

Instant coffee and water

"The water turns brown".

Vinegar and bicarbonate of soda

"There is lots of fizzing". "It looks as if a gas is coming off."

How do you explain what you see?

Nathan said: "I can see that sand and water do not mix or react. Sand is heavier than water and sinks to the bottom."

Ali said: "I can see the coffee mixes in and dissolves in the water as the coffee grains are no longer visible."

Mina said: "Vinegar and bicarbonate of soda seem to react to each other. I can see a gas coming off which means a new substance is being made."

React

When materials undergo a chemical change to make new materials.

Bicarbonate of soda

A white solid used in baking and fizzy drinks to reduce acidity.

Test your learning

On track

1 Look carefully at the observations and explanations Mina, Ali and Nathan made.

(a) Write down the names of the two liquids they used.

(b) Write down the names of the three solids they used.

(c) Write down the letter of the one where a chemical reaction occurred.

Aiming higher

2 Mina mixed some more materials with water. Here are her observations.

Material	Observations
plaster of Paris	The mixture warms a little. After a short while the plaster of Paris powder makes a new, hard solid which sinks to the bottom.
salt and water	After a little while the salt seems to "disappear into the water". You can't see it any more.
glass beads and water	The glass beads settle on the bottom of the jar. Nothing else seems to happen.

(a) Which material dissolves in water? Use the table to explain why.

(b) Which material reacts with water? Use the table to explain why.

(c) Which material does not react or dissolve in water? Use the table to explain why.

How well am I doing?

On track

I can describe some changes that might happen when materials are added to water.

Aiming higher

I can use observations to make sense of the results.

19 How can you separate solids from liquids?

- There are many different kinds of filters.
- **Filtering** helps separate undissolved solids from a liquid.

Water in a stream is dirty. It has stones and sand in it, as well as other pollutants. How can you separate the solids out? The answer is to use a sieve. A piece of cloth or even a pair of tights will do. Treating it further might make it safe to drink.

What kind of filters are there?

Gardeners often use riddles. This doesn't mean they joke a lot! A riddle is a coarse sieve with very large holes, used to separate stones from soil.

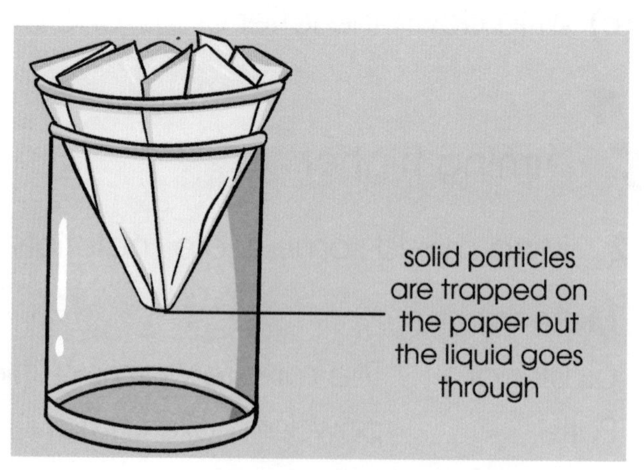

Scientists use folded filter paper. These are like sieves but the holes are very small. Special paper is used.

How do filters work?

The garden riddle works because the little pieces of soil can fall through the holes and the big stones stay trapped in the sieve.

The filter paper is a similar idea. The holes let the liquid trickle through but any solids, such as filter coffee, are trapped on the paper.

Riddle

Another word for a garden sieve.

Mesh

A knitted material with small holes in it.

Test your learning

On track

1 Leopard class had some equipment. They used it to see how well a mixture of marbles, water and very fine sand could be **filtered**.

kitchen colander (large holes)

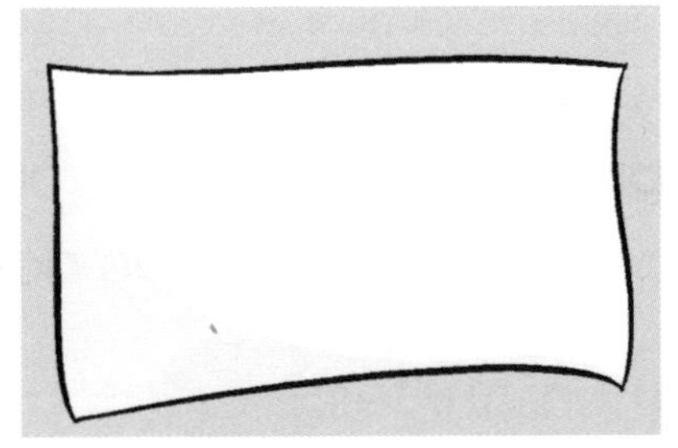

blotting paper (very small holes)

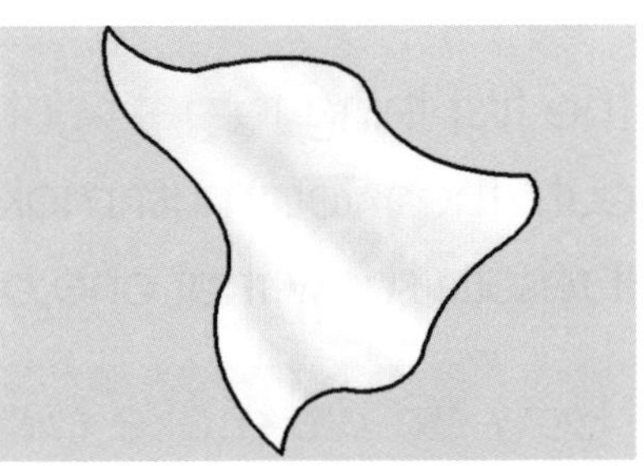

muslin (medium-sized holes)

Here are some predictions Leopard class made before they used the equipment.

1 Only the marbles will be filtered out.

2 All the marbles and sand will be filtered out.

3 All the marbles will be filtered out and most of the sand.

(a) Match the predictions to the correct piece of equipment.

Aiming higher

2 Ali had some water with sand and stones in it. He wanted to have just pure water.

(a) He tried to filter it using a sieve with large holes. Explain what happened.

(b) Then he used filter paper. Explain what happened this time.

How well am I doing?

On track

I can name a few types of filters and what they do.

Aiming higher

I can describe how filters work.

20 What are the stages in a test?

- **Tests start with a question and end when you can make sense of your results.**
- **Your results will show if your prediction is correct or not.**

The first thing to get right in a test is the question: What do you want to find out? Then you must make **predictions** and carry out a test to check them. If results show that one of them is right, you have done your job.

How do we make a start on our test?

Mr Sharma first asked his class this question:

Next Nathan and Ali made some predictions.

Whose prediction was right?

Nathan and Ali then came up with a way of testing their predictions.

"We shall have to add some salt to water and wait for it all to dissolve. Then we'll filter it through a filter paper in a funnel. We'll look at what happens and taste any liquid that passes through."

Nathan observed there were no salt crystals on the paper. He was disappointed. It looked as if his prediction did not fit the observations.

Ali realised that because there was no salt on the paper, it must have passed through in the liquid. He was pleased. His prediction fitted this observation.

Mr Sharma said, "Well done – you have found out you cannot get salt from salty water by filtering."

Observation
Something you see happening.

Fact
Something that is true to start with.

Test your learning

On track

1 Nathan realised he could think about his test in different steps. He wrote down the different steps but in the wrong order.

- See if the results match the prediction or not.
- Make observations.
- Decide how to do the test.
- Think of a question to test.
- Make sense of the results.
- Carry out the test.
- Make a prediction.

(a) Write out the steps in the right order.

Aiming higher

2 Jessica wrote down four statements about a similar test using sugar.

1 Can you get sugar back from a sugary solution by filtering?
2 I know that sugar dissolves in water.
3 All the sugar solution goes through the filter paper.
4 It will not be possible to separate sugar from sugary water.

(a) Which statement is a fact?

(b) Which statement is a question to test?

(c) Which statement is a prediction?

(d) Which observation in the list shows the prediction to be correct?

How well am I doing?

On track

I can tell you the different stages of one scientific test.

Aiming higher

I can use observations to say if a prediction is correct or not.

21 How are forces measured?

- **Forces** are measured using a **Newton meter**.
- The **Newton (N)** is the only correct unit of force and weight.

Newton meters (sometimes called force meters) measure the size of **forces**. The spring inside gets longer as the force pulling it gets bigger. Forces are measured in units called **Newtons**. Weight is a force. An apple weighs about 1 Newton.

How does a Newton meter work?

This Newton meter has a spring inside which stretches evenly as weights are added to it. The stronger they pull, the longer the spring becomes. A marker (or pointer) on the end of the spring points to the right weight.

This meter can read from 0 N to 10 N. Others can read to 100 N or even 500 N.

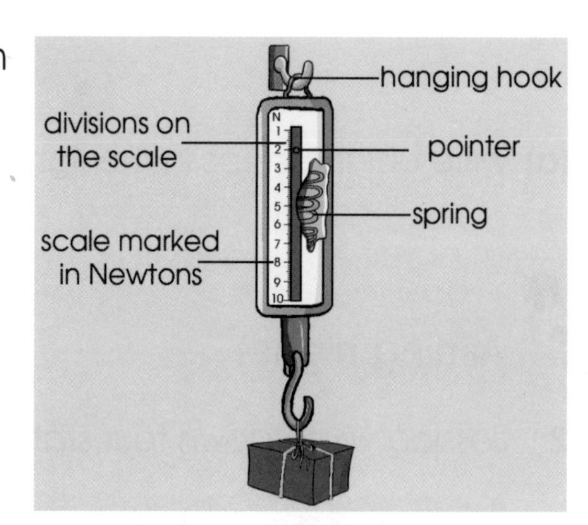

Can we compare different skeletons?

Newtons are the units of force. Forces are pushes and pulls.

Gravity pulls Ali's small apple down. The Newton meter only measures 1 Newton.

Compared to the apple, Ali is very big. Gravity is pulling down on the weighing scales with a force of 300 Newtons.

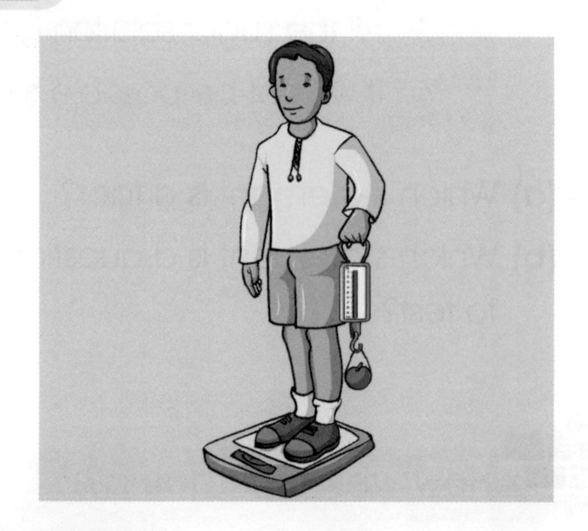

Stretch

To get longer.

Weight

The downward force on an object caused by gravity.

Test your learning

On track

1 Mina wanted to weigh five apples on the scale. It has a spring inside it, just like a Newton meter.

(a) For five apples, what would the reading be on the scale?

(b) What would be the reading on the scale if you put another three apples in the pan?

(c) What else could you use to weigh the apples?

Aiming higher

2 Jessica used a Newton meter to lift or pull several objects. She put her results in a table.

Object and action	Force needed
lifting a pencil case	1
pulling a toy across the	4
lifting a bucket	10
pulling a door open	6

(a) What units did Jessica measure the forces in?

(b) Which of the objects was hardest to move or lift?

How well am I doing?

On track

I can name what we need to use to measure forces.

Aiming higher

I can use the units of force, Newtons, correctly.

22 Can friction be useful?

- **Friction** happens when two materials rub against each other.
- Both low and high friction can be useful.

You might come across a force called **friction**. This is the force between two surfaces rubbing together. Friction tries to slow things down. It is high if the surfaces are dry and rough, and it is low if the surfaces are smooth and wet.

What kinds of surface produce the most friction?

Friction is caused when two materials rub against each other. Rough surfaces usually produce more friction than smooth ones.

The car stops quickly. The dry, rough surface of the road and the tyres make lots of friction.

The car takes a long time to slow down. The icy road is smooth and reduces the friction.

Is friction useful?

Here is what Leopard class said.

Sometimes it's useful to have a lot of friction. For example, goalkeepers' gloves are rough and help them grip the ball.

Having little friction can also be useful. Playground slides are smooth. They help you slide quickly and safely. If they were rough they would hurt you.

Friction
The force produced when two materials rub against each other.

Surface
The uppermost part of a material.

Test your learning

On track

1 Mina made a collection of different materials. Some had smooth and some had rough surfaces.

ice

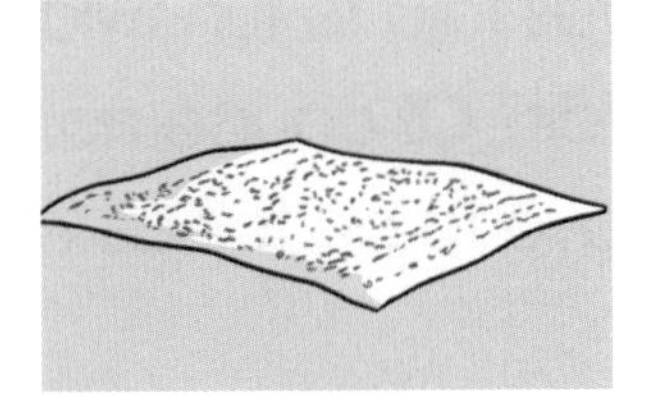
sandpaper

glass

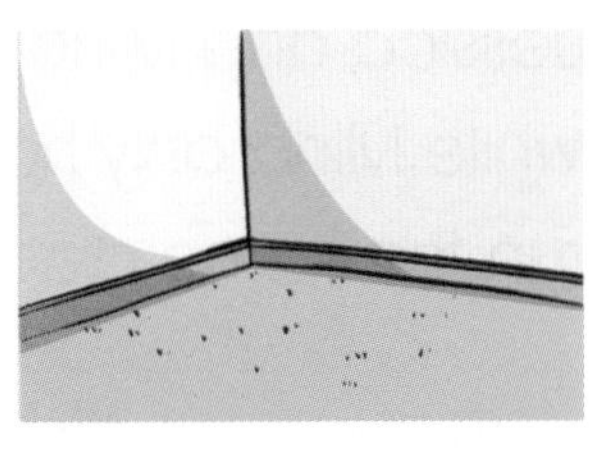
carpet

(a) Which of the surfaces would have "high friction" and which "low friction" when you rub them with your hand?

(b) Write down two more surfaces that might have "high friction" when you rub them with your hand.

Aiming higher

2 Mina drew up a list of everyday examples where friction is helpful.

swimming	a car engine working smoothly
roller skating	walking
tying your shoelaces	a fighter plane flying fast
pulling a drawer out of a desk	holding your bicycle handlebars

(a) Decide if it is important for friction to be high or low in each example. Rewrite the list, putting them into these two groups.

(b) Give one way in which friction can be reduced.

How well am I doing?

On track

I can explain what friction is and when it happens.

Aiming higher

I can describe examples where friction can be helpful.

23 How do you test for friction?

- You can investigate which surfaces produce the most friction.
- Some **tests are fair**, others are not.

Jessica and Mina had a race. Jessica was told to run twice around the track, while Mina only had to go once. Is that fair? Of course not. They must both run the same distance. Scientific tests have to be fair as well.

What ideas did Ali have?

Ali had to test the question: Does an object slide most easily on smooth surfaces?

He had some ideas to help him plan his test and he made a prediction.

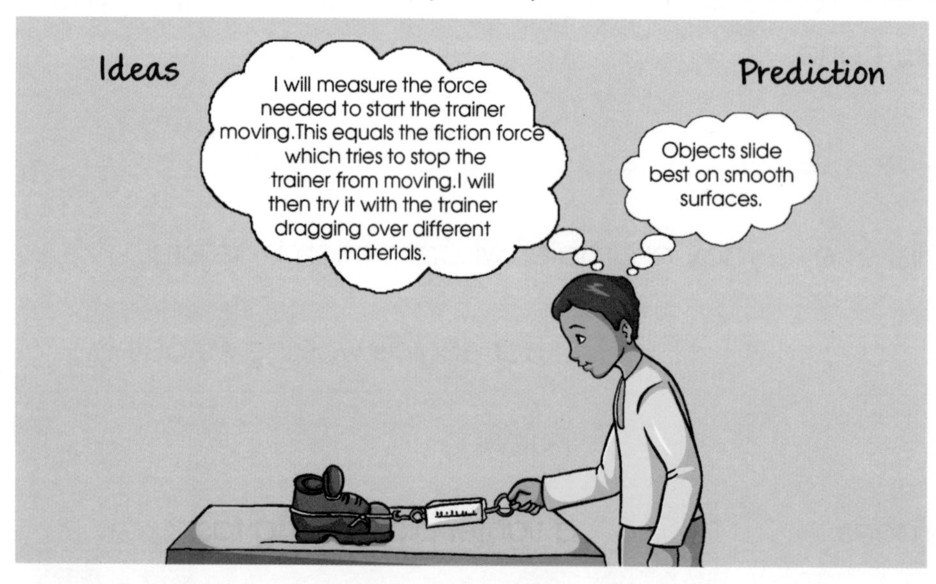

How did Ali make sure his test was fair?

Ali pulled his trainer across the table with a Newton meter.

He measured the force needed to make his trainer start moving.

He changed the surface. He pulled his trainer again and measured how the force changed.

His test was fair because he used the same trainer every time.

Force

A push, pull, twist or turn.

Fair test

A scientific investigation that is reliable.

Test your learning

On track

1 Here is some equipment Ali might have used in his test to see if an object slides most easily on a smooth surface.

(a) What pieces of equipment would Ali **not** need in his test? Explain your answer.

(b) What measurements would he take?

Aiming higher

2 Ali thought about the factors in his **fair test**. He drew a table.

What I kept the same	What I changed	What I measured

(a) Draw a table just like Ali's. Complete it by adding:

1. the factor Ali kept the same in his test
2. the factor he changed
3. what he measured.

(b) What is the name of the force that makes it hard for the trainer to start moving?

(c) What units would he use when measuring the force on his Newton meter?

How well am I doing?

On track

I can describe how you can investigate friction.

Aiming higher

I can describe how to do a fair test.

24 How do we show results clearly?

- **Information needs to be organised well.**
- **Tables and bar charts help you make sense of test results.**

Once you have got your data you can see if it makes sense. Organising your results in a **table** or a **bar chart** makes it easier to spot any patterns. You can use your chart or table to say if your prediction was accurate or not.

What results did Ali get?

Do you remember Ali's prediction? "Objects slide best on smooth surfaces."

In his test he tried four different surfaces. These are the results he got.

Surface 1 (carpet)	20 N on the Newton meter
Surface 2 (plastic sheet)	4 N on the Newton meter
Surface 3 (sandpaper)	15 N on the Newton meter
Surface 4 (cloth)	10 N on the Newton meter

How did Ali use the results?

Material	Smoothness of material	How easily does the trainer slide?	Force measured on the Newton meter
plastic sheet	smoothest	very easily	4 N
cloth	slightly rough		10 N
sandpaper	quite rough		15 N
carpet	roughest	not easily	20 N

Ali put his results in a table. To make the pattern clearer, he put the results in order of size. You can see that the smoothest material has the lowest friction and slides the easiest, so the force needed to move the trainer is the lowest. Ali had made a good prediction.

Information

A collection of facts.

Bar chart

A graph with vertical bars which show the size of a measurement.

Test your learning

On track

1 Ali did a second test and tested some other materials in the same way. He put his results in a bar chart.

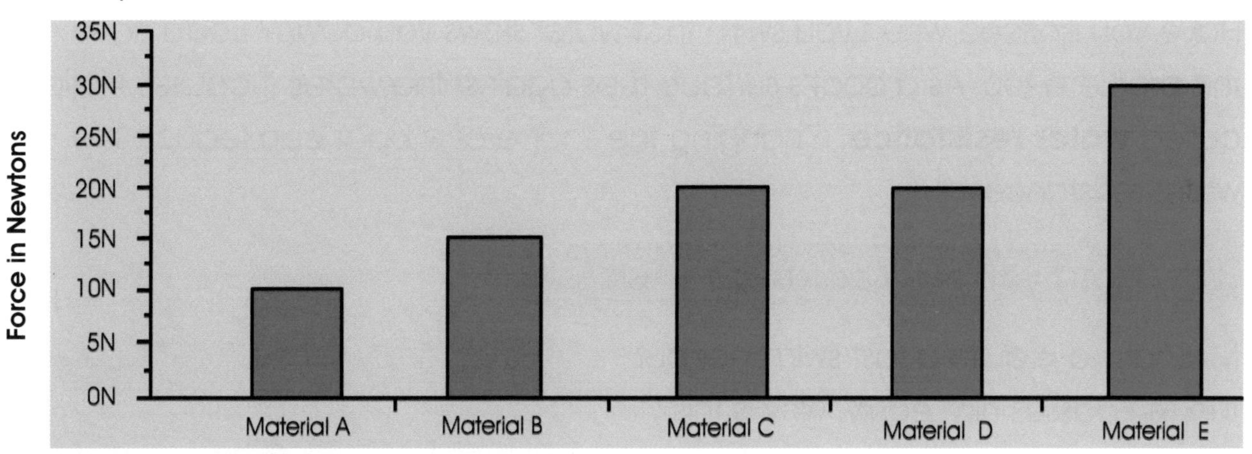

(a) Which material does the trainer slide over most easily?

(b) Which two materials produced the same amount of friction?

(c) Use the bar chart to make a table of Ali's second set of results.

Aiming higher

2 Ali tried some other materials. Here are his results.

Material	Smoothness of material	Force of friction
F	smoothest	2N
G		10N
H		25N
I		20N
J	roughest	35N

(a) What pattern does the table show?

(b) Which reading looks odd? Explain why you think it is.

How well am I doing?

On track

I know some good ways to show my results.

Aiming higher

I can use my results to make sense of my test.

25 What is water resistance?

- **Objects are slowed down in water by water resistance.**
- **Some shapes move more quickly through water than others.**

Have you noticed when you swim that water slows you down? Boats have this problem too. As a boat's surface rubs against the water, it causes friction called **water resistance**. Changing the shape of a boat can reduce the water resistance.

Why can't you swim as fast as a fish?

Mr Sharma is quite a fast swimmer but the fish passes him easily. Why is this?

The **water resistance** slows him down because he is the wrong shape. If he was a different shape he could go much faster.

Why is a submarine the shape it is?

A submarine moves easily through water because:

- it is streamlined
- the rounded prow and curved conning tower help it glide though the water
- the smooth surface reduces "rub"
- special paint on the hull also reduces friction.

All this reduces the water resistance.

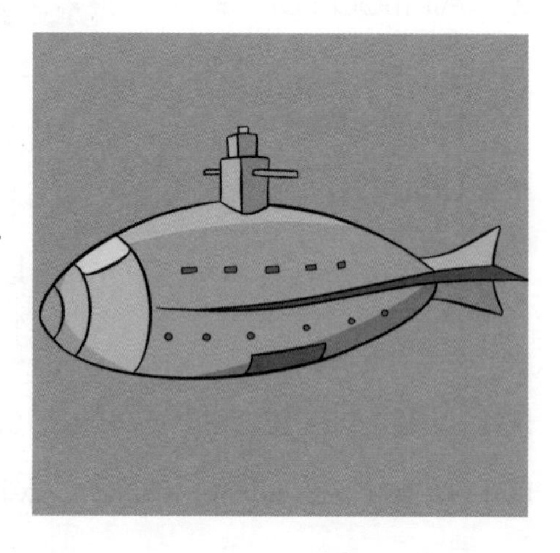

Prow
The front end of a boat.

Hull
The main body of a boat.

Test your learning

On track

1 This is the largest ship in the world. It is called the *Emma Maersk*.

(a) What is the name of the force which slows the ship moving through the water?

(b) Explain why anybody would want that force to be less?

The *Emma Maersk*

Aiming higher

2 Jessica dropped four pieces of plasticine into a cylinder of water. They were all the same weight but their shapes were different. She timed how long it took in seconds for each one to reach the bottom.

	Shape 1	Shape 2	Shape 3	Shape 4
Time it took to fall	0.55 s	1.0 s	1.5 s	2.5 s

(a) Explain why Jessica's test was fair.

(b) Jessica predicted: "The plasticine that is the most streamlined will fall the quickest." Do her results confirm this?

How well am I doing?

On track

I can explain what water resistance is.

Aiming higher

I can explain the link between shape and water resistance.

26 Why do some electrical circuits not work?

- **Circuits need a source of electrical power to work.**
- **Circuits might not work for a variety of reasons.**

Cells or **batteries** are good, safe sources of electrical power. Circuits that work all have a power source, materials that conduct electricity joined in a circuit, no gaps and a component like a bulb or motor.

What do cells do?

Jessica said, "The chemicals in cells make electricity, to give a circuit the power to make them work. Two or more cells joined together are a **battery** of cells, or just a battery."

"Circuits do not work if the cells are connected wrongly. Always put the + **terminal** of one cell to the – **terminal** of the next. Never connect two + or two – terminals."

cells correctly connected

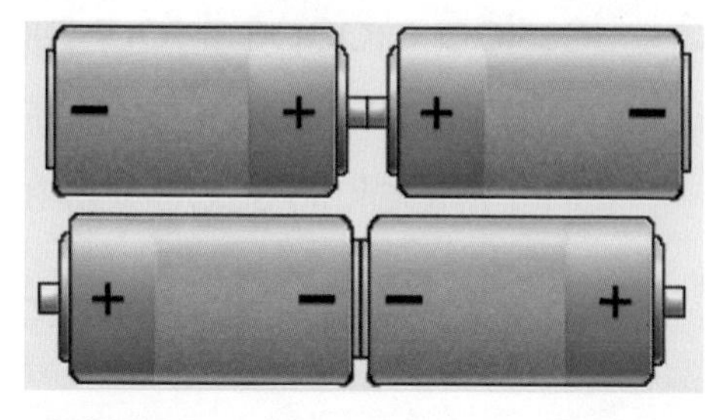

cells wrongly connected

Why do some circuits not work?

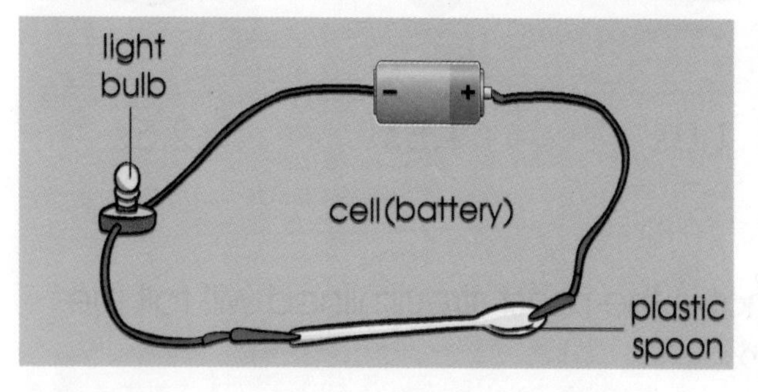

This does not work as the plastic spoon is an electrical insulator.

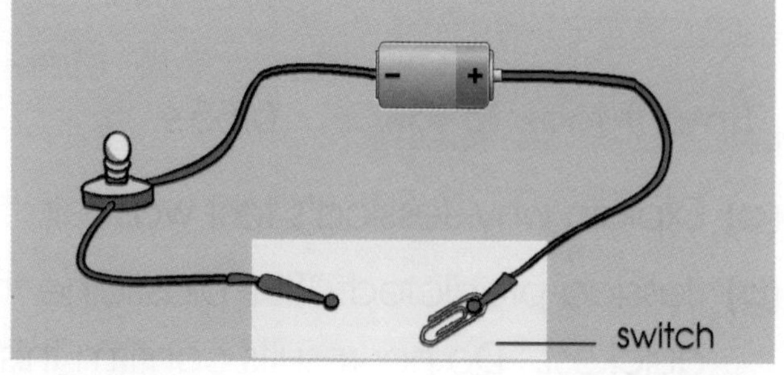

This does not work as the open switch leaves a gap in the circuit.

Cell

A device which provides electricity for a circuit to work.

Battery

Made by joining two or more electrical cells together.

Test your learning

On track

1 Jessica had a brand new torch. It holds two cells joined together as a battery. It wasn't working.

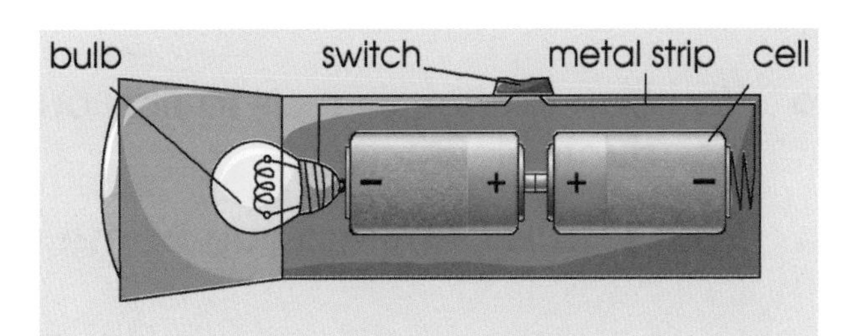

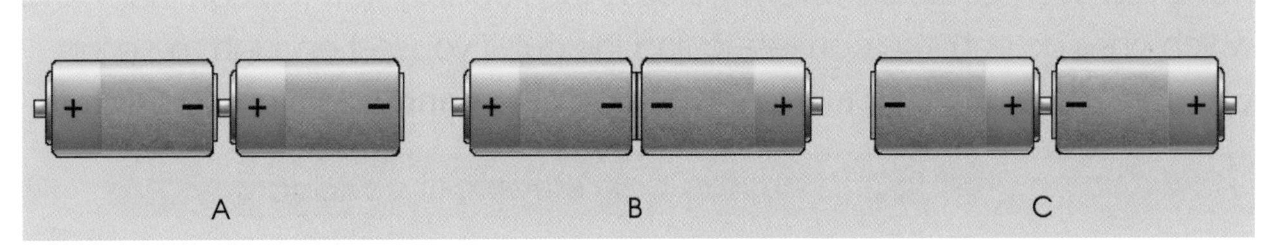

(a) What do the cells (batteries) do in the torch circuit?

(b) What should Jessica have done to make her torch work?

(c) Which of the arrangements of cells above (A, B and C) will work in her torch?

Aiming higher

2 Jessica made a circuit. Unfortunately it did not work.

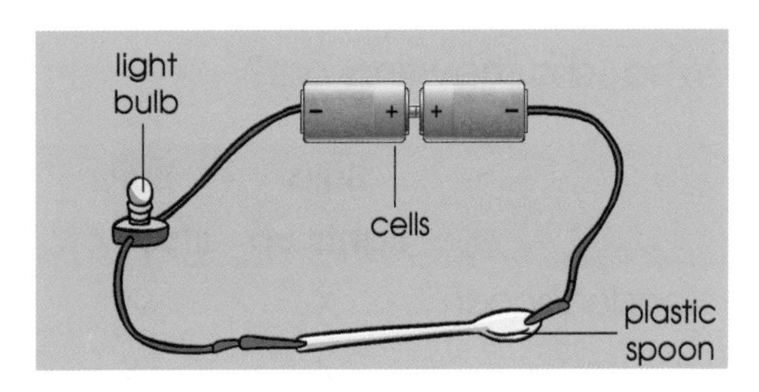

(a) Write down two reasons why Jessica's circuit might not have worked.

(b) Draw the circuit after she fixed it.

How well am I doing?

On track

I can say what cells or batteries do in a circuit.

Aiming higher

I can give three reasons why some circuits might not work.

27 Which materials let electricity pass through?

- You can do simple tests to find out if a material conducts electricity.
- Your results can help you come up with a rule.

Have you ever wondered which materials let electricity flow through them and which ones do not? You can test to find this out. If you test enough materials, you can come up with a rule to group them into **conductors** and **insulators**.

How can you test to find out the best electrical conductors?

Some materials let electricity flow through them and are called **electrical conductors**. Others don't and are called **electrical insulators**. Jessica and Ali set up a circuit with two cells, a bulb and some wires. There was a gap in the circuit. The bulb lit up when some materials were put in the gap.

What did they find out?

	Bulb lights up	Bulb stays off
wooden spoon	✗	✓
kitchen foil	✓	✗
metal fork	✓	✗
plastic comb	✗	✓
paperclip	✓	✗
rubber	✗	✓

Jessica said: "The bulb lights up when metals are connected but stays off when the material is a non-metal."

Ali came up with a rule. "Metals are good **electrical conductors** and non-metals are good **electrical insulators**."

Electrical conductor
A material which lets electricity flow through it easily.

Electrical insulator
A material which electricity finds it hard to flow through.

Test your learning

On track

1 Jessica had a closer look at the wires they used in their circuit.

She noticed it was made out of two different materials.

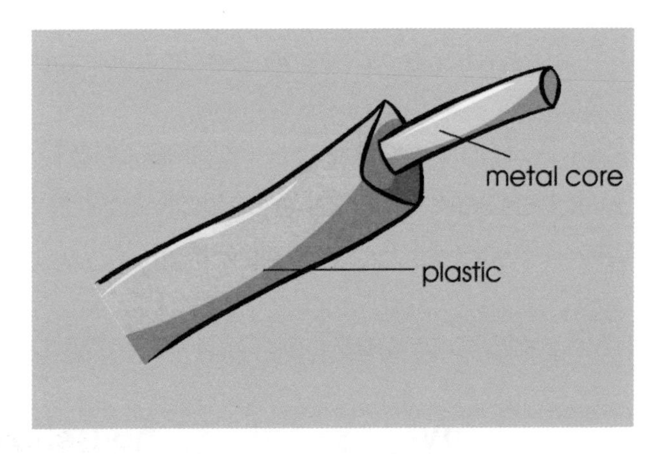

(a) Which part of the wire is made out of an electrical conductor?

(b) Explain why the wire is covered with plastic.

Aiming higher

2 Jessica and Nathan tested some more materials to see if they conducted electricity.

feather

metal key

a ring pull

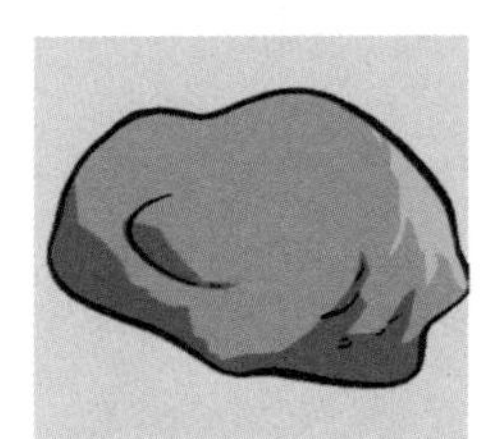
stone

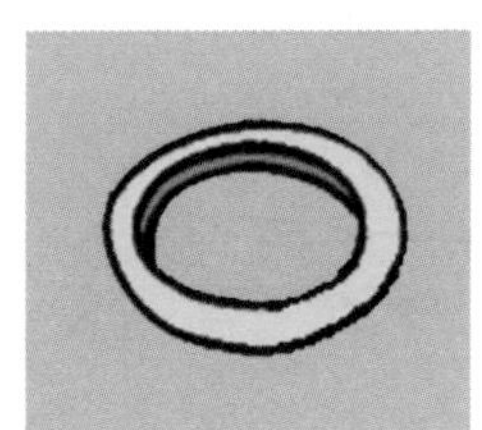
gold ring

(a) Use their rule to sort the materials into electrical conductors and insulators.

(b) Write down the names of two more materials that are electrical conductors and two that are electrical insulators.

How well am I doing?

On track

I can describe how to test to see if a material conducts electricity.

Aiming higher

I can use a rule to say if a material might conduct electricity or not.

28 How do switches work?

- **Many household devices have a switch.**
- **All switches work in basically the same way.**

Your TV, lights, washing machine and DVD recorder all have an **on/off switch**. Switches save a lot of electricity by turning the device off when it is not in use. When switches are on, electricity flows around the circuit and the devices work.

Why do devices have on/off switches?

TV	household lights	washing machine
DVD recorder	Play Station	computer

All of these household devices have a switch that turns the device on and off. This saves a lot of electricity by turning the device off when it is not in use.

How easy is it to make a simple switch?

Look at how these switches have been made out of everyday materials.

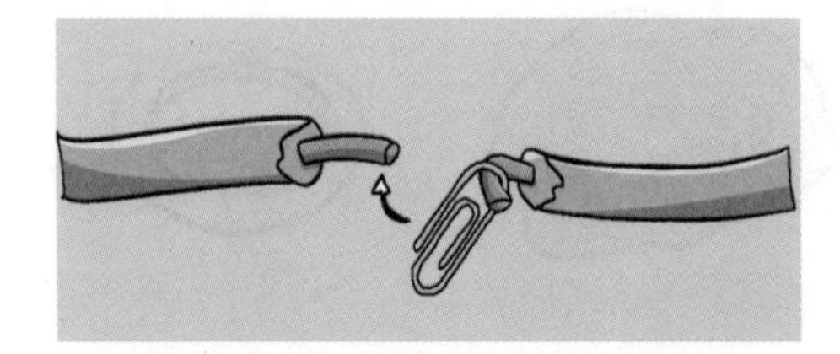

The paperclip acts here as a switch. It links on to one wire. As you see it the switch is open. If the paperclip moves to touch the other wire, the switch closes and electricity flows.

This switch has a springy strip of metal. The picture shows it open. If you press it down onto the drawing pin, the circuit will be completed and electricity will flow through.

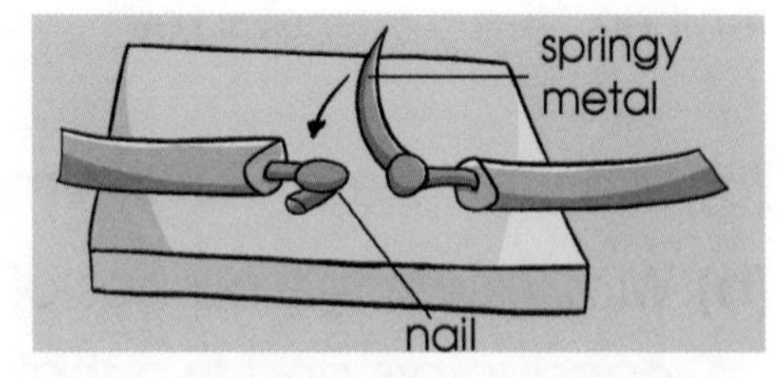

This switch has wires fixed with paper fasteners onto a piece of card. The other side of the card has some metal foil attached. When the card is pressed together the switch is on.

Switch
A device which switches a circuit on and off.

Device
A piece of equipment like a television or a computer.

Test your learning

On track

1 Here are some things you might have in your home.

(a) Which two items have switches in them?

(b) Give a good reason why it is useful for a device to have an on/off switch.

Aiming higher

2 Look at this circuit. It has a switch in it.

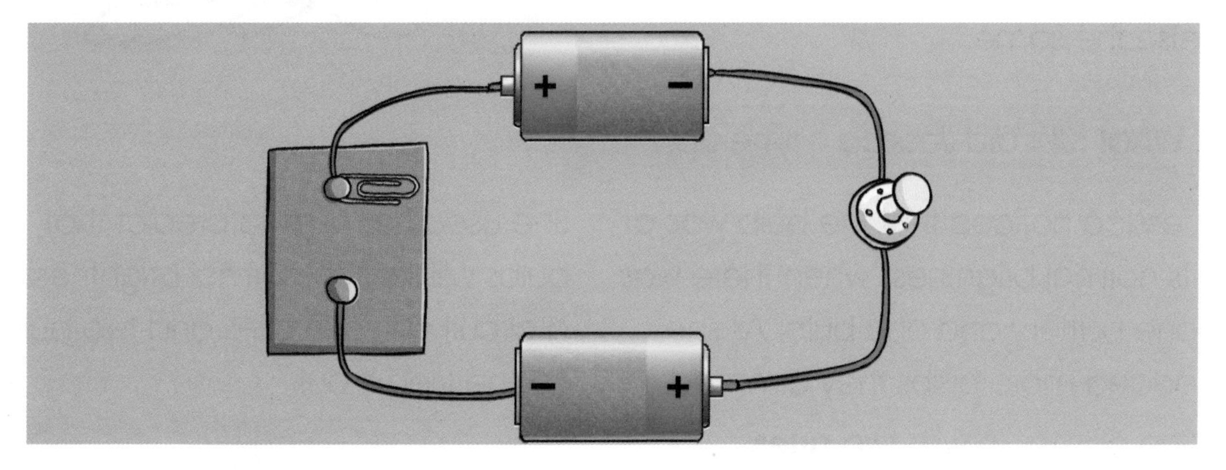

(a) The switch is open. What will happen in the circuit?

(b) What will happen in the circuit when the switch is closed?

(c) Describe in your own words how a switch works.

How well am I doing?

On track

I can name five household devices from memory that contain a switch.

Aiming higher

I can describe how a switch works.

29 What affects how brightly a bulb lights up?

- **Fair tests help you find out the "brightness rule".**
- **Once you know the rule you can make more predictions.**

You can test different circuits to find out how changing the number of bulbs and cells affects the **brightness**. You can come up with a **rule** that helps you predict what might happen in a circuit you have not made yet. That's clever science!

What experiments did Jessica do to test the "brightness rule"?

Jessica wanted to find out how she might change the brightness of a bulb.

To make her circuits easy to compare, Jessica decided to change the number of bulbs and keep everything else the same.

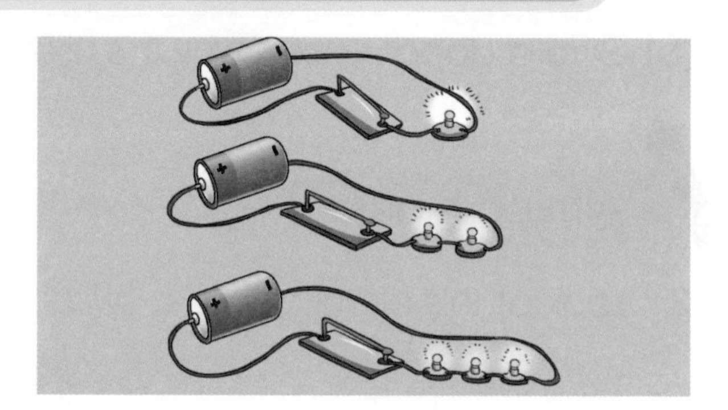

What rule did Jessica come up with?

Jessica noticed that the bulb was at its normal brightness when there was one battery and one bulb. As she added more bulbs they dimmed.

She came up with two **rules**.

"If the number of bulbs and cells are the same, the brightness will be normal."

"The bulbs will be dimmer than normal if there are more bulbs than cells."

She used her rules to predict that bulbs will light to normal brightness in a circuit with two cells and two bulbs. So she tried it out.

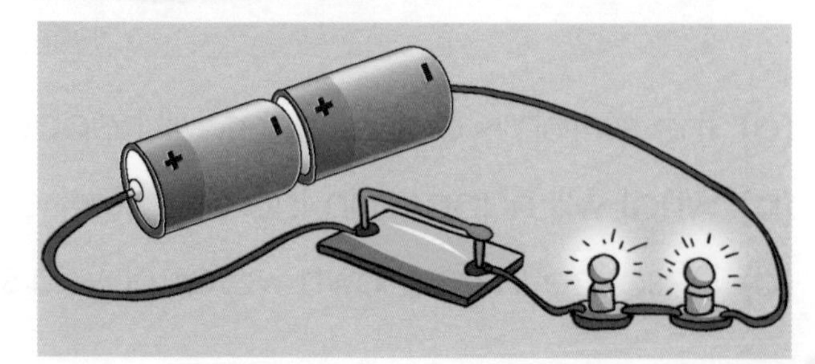

She was right. It was a good rule.

Factor

That which you keep the same, or observe changing in a fair test.

Fair test

A scientific way of finding out a pattern, rule or scientific law.

Test your learning

On track

1 Jessica thought more about her test.

	What she kept the same	What she changed	What she observed
number of bulbs			
type of bulb			
number of cells			
brightness of the bulb(s)			

(a) What question did Jessica test?

(b) Copy out the table and tick the correct boxes.

Aiming higher

2 Jessica then tested another rule. "The bulbs will be brighter than normal if there are more batteries than bulbs."

	What she kept the same	What she changed	What she observed
number of bulbs			
type of bulb			
number of cells			
brightness of the bulb(s)			

(a) Copy the table. Tick the correct boxes to make Jessica's second test fair.

(b) Draw the circuits she might have made.

(c) Label them to show the names of the parts.

How well am I doing?

On track

I can design a fair test.

Aiming higher

I can use the "brightness rule" correctly to make predictions.

Index